PATRICK CHUDI OKAFOR

Alternate Route to
School Effectiveness and
Student Achievement

Circumventing Socioeconomic Status

iUniverse, Inc.
Bloomington

Alternate Route to School Effectiveness and Student Achievement
Circumventing Socioeconomic Status

Copyright © 2012 Patrick Chudi Okafor

iUniverse books may be ordered through booksellers or by contacting:

iUniverse
1663 Liberty Drive
Bloomington, IN 47403
www.iuniverse.com
1-800-Authors (1-800-288-4677)

Because of the dynamic nature of the Internet, any Web addresses or
links contained in this book may have changed since publication and
may no longer be valid. The views expressed in this work are solely those
of the author and do not necessarily reflect the views of the publisher,
and the publisher hereby disclaims any responsibility for them.

Any people depicted in stock imagery provided by Thinkstock are models,
and such images are being used for illustrative purposes only.

Certain stock imagery © Thinkstock.

ISBN: 978-1-4759-3045-0 (sc)
ISBN: 978-1-4759-3047-4 (hc)
ISBN: 978-1-4759-3046-7 (e)

Printed in the United States of America

iUniverse rev. date: 6/26/2012

CONTENTS

LIST OF TABLES

LIST OF FIGURES

Acknowledgement

This is a revised and updated copy of my dissertation on *School climate, pupil control ideology and effectiveness*. I continue to thank my mentors and the faculty of the School of Education, St. John's University, New York, for their support and encouragement. My gratitude also goes to Dr. Chux Cornelius Okochi (Adjunct assistant professor, St. John's University, New York), for accepting to write the foreword to this book.

Dedication

This book is dedicated to children who cannot afford education, and to those children who do not have access to education.

FOREWORD

"Are the successes and failures of pupils destined on their parent's income, educational attainment and neighborhood? Are children from low socioeconomic status background destined to fail, both in academics and in future status in adult life?" These among others, led the author to offer solutions to the issue of failure associated with low socioeconomic status, just as more children fall within this bracket and as the gap between the rich and the poor continues to widen. A learning environment is a strong stimulus for societal change, development and growth. Dr. Patrick Chudi Okafor portrayed this fact in this book based on research conducted within New York City public schools, in which he examined climate as an alternate route to school effectiveness and student academic achievement and a way to circumvent socioeconomic status.

Many authors starting from Coleman and colleagues (1966) pointed to family's low socioeconomic status as the culprit in students' failures. Dr. Okafor in this book returns the focus to the school as an easier way out, when he asked: "isn't the improvement of school climate a less difficult route to school effectiveness and student's academic achievement? Isn't it much easier to change schooling, teaching and learning than to change parent's income, educational attainment and neighborhood?" By so doing the author justified the need for this study, and the necessity for the improvement of the general school climate whose focus is on teaching and learning and school effectiveness.

The evolvement of any strategic plan for school improvement should therefore take consideration of school climate which is the means for quality input and the goal for greater output or school effectiveness as stated by the author. The main actors in an open, healthy and humanistic school climate or school environment are the students, teachers and principals and these should be involved in harmonious interrelationship for school improvement and students academic achievement as pointed by the author. By basing his studies in an area with low socioeconomic status Dr. Okafor attempted to, according to him "disprove the myth that low socioeconomic status is a panacea for either failure in school or in adult life; that failure should not be seen as a destiny; that there is redemption and the school has a major role to play". By using the worst case scenarios of inner city schools and marginal groups as examples the author tried to make this work a handbook for all who care about educational improvement of their wards, no matter how academically impoverished they are.

John Dewey spoke of the importance of the term 'environment' for a sound philosophy of education. "It must be seen to be dominantly human and its values as social. Through the influence of the social environment each person becomes saturated with the customs, the beliefs, the purposes, skills, hopes and fears of the cultural group to which he belongs. The features of even his physical surroundings come to him through the eyes and ears of the community" (John Dewey. The Need for a Philosophy of Education; in <u>Developmental Counseling and Teaching</u> by Erickson & Whiteley, Brooks/Cole Publishing Company, California: 1980; p.7).

In many years of classroom experience, I have come to realize that education is more than simply imparting knowledge, but building bridges of life. Each piece of the bridge is connected to the other through the richness and thrust emanating from what each student brings from home and what the school offers. By basing the overarching framework of his study on openness of the school and family systems, the author justifies the saying that 'it takes a village to raise a child' when he clearly stated that, "The school and the home as open systems must work together towards the acquisition and the fostering of the academic and social capital needed by a child for academic achievement. The academic relationship between the home and the school must be improved to guarantee sustainable student academic performance". Consequently, the author shifted responsibility also to the family or what he called "the home climate", as a major contributor to what children bring to school.

Success hinges on the understanding that we need a great doze of openness and motivation in approaching the student-filled environment. Our current society harbors many individuals who have achieved academic excellence and success in life despite their low socioeconomic upbringing; all depended so much on the type of openness, motivation and support available to them in their years of academic pursuit, even when their economic background was so low. Some schools in poor neighborhoods have defied the demographics of low socioeconomic status to achieve success. This book attests to these factors and should serve as a tribute to each and every one of those persons in our world today engaged in promoting an environment that is open, healthy and humanistic for learning, which emphasizes academic development.

Chux Cornelius Okochi, Ph D, MA
Adjunct Assistant Professor
St. John's University, Queens, New York

What's the Fuss about Socioeconomic Status and Academic Achievement?

Eric is a 10 year old white male student in a fourth-grade class in a public school located in a minority neighborhood in the Northeastern part of the U.S. The school's ethnic compositions are 54 percent Blacks, 33 percent Latinos, 6 percent Whites and 7 percent Asians. Eric has been placed back in his home after being in a foster care for 2 years. His father is in the state penitentiary for the past 4 years for steeling computer parts and for domestic abuse. His mother a recovering drug addict works at the local grocery store in the morning and at the car wash in the evening to support herself and her child. The school which Eric attends has a high student teacher ratio and large class sizes, meaning less individual attention for each student. The school library has older and fewer books; the school building and school play ground are poorly maintained, the classrooms have poorly maintained infrastructures. Eric's school environment is less motivating for learning; teachers are less qualified, less experienced and less paid; they have low student expectation; teachers in this school complain that most of their students are troublemakers who are disruptive during learning. The principal rarely visits the classrooms; she is always busy in her office, sometimes visiting the school board for one problem or the other; there are fewer extracurricular activities; students have less access to the school nurses and social workers. Eric has no friend in school, no kid wants to be his friend; his teacher says 'he is disruptive and disrespectful in class'; other kids make fun of him. Eric and his mom live in a challenging neighborhood where they have to deal with drug and gun violence.

The grocery stores in this neighborhood have a lot of junk food, there are rarely a store where one can buy fruits and vegetables, and a good one is about 8 miles away in a better neighborhood. Eric gets home to a mom who is tired from her first job, and has to leave him to the care of her neighbor for her evening job at the car wash. Eric comes from a background of low socioeconomic status.

Since the alarming report of Coleman and associates (1966) on the impact of the home, neighborhood and peer environment on a child's educational achievement and the lingering effect of these on the child's social status in adult life, socioeconomic status (SES) has taken a central place in academic studies. These authors found that economic and social class was a major determinant of educational achievement and future success in adult life. Among all the variables for determining students' academic performance, socioeconomic status became prominent, and as such, every educational processes and outcomes were increasingly predicated on socioeconomic criteria (Bornstein & Bradley, 2003; St. John, 1970). High socioeconomic status presumably became the cure-all for academic achievement among academic researchers and scholars, leading this author to ask these questions: Are the successes and failures of pupils destined on their parent's income, educational attainment and neighborhood? Are children from low socioeconomic status background destined to fail, both in academics and in future status in adult life? Is it then a waste of time to send children to school?

What is socioeconomic status? It was described as the hierarchical ranking of an individual or a family in terms of possession and influence over wealth, power and social status (Mueller & Parcel, 1981). Nevertheless, there is no single agreed upon definition of socioeconomic status among researchers, though, many tend to agree, that it incorporates parental income, education, and occupation (Gottfried, 1985; Houser, 1994).

The primacy of socioeconomic status criteria was assumed and unchallenged until the meta-analytical research of White (1982) on the relationship between socioeconomic status and academic achievement; and by a follow up research by Sirin (2005). The findings of these aforementioned authors showed that there is more to socioeconomic status than generally assumed. White (1982) found a weak correlation between the traditional measures of socioeconomic status and academic achievement, but a strong correlation with grade level and home environment. Although Sirin's result showed an average to strong correlation between socioeconomic status and academic achievement, these were mediated by a number of factors. Sirin also found that the traditional socioeconomic status categories (parental income, occupation, and education) were less predictive of academic achievement than other factors for minority students.

In their correlation and multiple regression analytical study (involving school climate, socioeconomic status and students achievement), Hoy and Sabo (1998) found that the dimensions of school climate had significant but independent effects on academic achievement; cumulatively they appear to rival socioeconomic status. In his doctoral dissertation in education at St. John's University New York this author provided additional validation for climate as a concept in its own right, as both the means and an end of school effectiveness. Having earned his doctorate, in the educational administration and supervision, this author is further providing further robust explanations of the predictive power and evaluative weight of the general school climates as having as much sway on student academic achievement as the known effects of socioeconomic status.

Socioeconomic status has been a good predictor of academic achievement and school effectiveness, but could not be easily manipulated or changed. Since it is easier to change school climate, than to alter students' socioeconomic statuses, isn't the improvement of school climate a less difficult route to school effectiveness and student academic achievement? Isn't it much easier to change schooling, teaching and learning than to change parent's income, educational attainment and neighborhood? Therefore, children's academic achievement should not be destined on their parents' socioeconomic statuses. Failure in adult life should not be a destiny for pupils of low socioeconomic background, when schools can do a better job.

In the above aforementioned studies of both White (1982) and Sirin (2005), certain factors of the home played mediating role in the relationship between socioeconomic status and academic achievement. White found that the home environment (among other socioeconomic status factors) has a strong relationship with academic achievement, and " is considerably more powerful than parents' income and education in influencing what children learn in the first six years of life and during the twelve years of primary and secondary education" (Walberg & Paik, 2000, p. 7). Consequently, the home environment could be isolated, as a more pliable alternative to student academic achievement, than parent income and education, among other socioeconomic factors. Hence, tinkering with the home environment, a major factor of socioeconomic status could be an additional way of breaking the jinx of failures associated with low socioeconomic status for low academic achieving pupils.

How then can the school and the family capitalize on the factors of the school (school climate) and those of home environment, which this author will call "home climate", for an integrative academic climate suitable for students' academic development? There have been many studies on the burden of low socioeconomic status for academic achievement, but few have proffered solution to the problem. Rather than discuss the problems, this author has undertaken to offer solution to the much discussed negative factors associated with low socioeconomic status and academic achievement.

The need for more inclusive studies investigating the dynamic properties of the school characterized by teacher-teacher, teacher-administrator, and teacher-student interactions, typified by climate calls for urgent attention (Hoy and Sabo, 1998; Willower & Jones, 1963).

In chapter one, the author began the book with a description of open system as the overarching framework of this work. The school and the family fall within the confines of open system; they are natural and conceived of social groups in interrelationships, and they are also rational and structured. They achieve their goals in a structured way within the larger environment from where they acquire resources. The aforementioned framework is significant in this study because as open systems, the school and the home must work together toward the acquisition and the fostering of the academic and social capital needed by a child for academic achievement. In this chapter, the author went further to explain the concepts of climates as openness and health and pupil control ideology, and that of effectiveness.

With examples from research done in public school in some states of the U.S., the author in chapter two went into the historical development of the concept, climate. Having given the reader an idea and understanding of what it means for a school to be open or closed, healthy or unhealthy, and the meaning of humanistic or custodial school ideology, the author went into the description of effectiveness as a good criterion for determining climate as both the means and an end of school survival, development and growth.

Since this study is based on data collected from public schools in New York City, the author in chapter three went into the propositions and the rationale for the interrelationships of climate as openness and health, pupil control ideology and their relationships to effectiveness. The aforesaid set the tone for the testing of the hypotheses and the result of the findings. The chapter on methodology and procedures for data collections, involving sampling, instrumentation and descriptive statistics was moved to the end of the book after the conclusion in order not to overwhelm the reader with academic and statistical issues, but still giving academic readers the opportunity to view the research methods in line with the traditional method of research.

In chapter four, the results of predicted hypotheses and unpredicted findings confirmed that climate is very significant for determining an open and healthy school, and for measuring a school with humanistic or custodial ideology. The result showed that an open and healthy school climate and a school with humanistic teacher-pupil control ideology is an effective school. It further demonstrated that among all climate elements, academic press or emphasis on academics is the catalyst or the sufficient condition for bringing about an effective school and for holding the climate elements together.

Chapter four further dealt with discussions of the findings, limitations and implications for policy, teaching and learning. Academic press or emphasis on academics, according to the findings is the core of school climate and a prerequisite for school effectiveness and student academic achievement. Academic press encapsulates the purpose, the major actors and activities of schooling. Climate was demonstrated as the means and end of school effectiveness, notwithstanding the fact that this research was conducted in New York City, an area with low socioeconomic status, as at the time of this study. This offers climate as a more feasible alternative to student academic achievement than socioeconomic status, which cannot be easily changed and altered. Therefore, it is much easier to change schooling, teaching and learning than to change parent's income, educational attainment and neighborhood.

In chapter five, the author examined further implication for educational policy, teaching and learning, shifting attention to what happens in school (teaching and learning) as paramount to student academic achievement. Responsibility was also apportioned to the family, the home climate, as a major determinant in what children bring to school. The author recommended liaison between school climate and home climate for an integrative students' academic development. Both the school and the family are contractual social open systems and the bedrocks of human relationships, exchanges, and interactions of shared orientations and shared ideologies (Appleberry & Hoy, 1979; Nwankwo, 1979). In this chapter, the author offered solution to the impact of low socioeconomic academic risk factors, and confronted all schools, teachers and parents, communities and governments on their roles in students' academic development and growth, and their responsibilities in enhancing teaching and learning.

The data for this study was collected from New York City public schools, an area with low socioeconomic status at the time of this study. Besides investigating climate in these schools as the means and end of schools' survival, development and growth or as a means of school effectiveness and by implication student's academic achievement, this author discusses the need to enhance school climate as bypass to socioeconomic status. Having based his study in an area with low socioeconomic status, this author attempted to disprove the myth that low socioeconomic status is a panacea for either failure in school or in adult life; that failure should not be seen as a destiny; that there is redemption and the school has a major role to play. The worst case scenario of inner city schools and marginal groups were used as data samples and examples to make this study an inference for other localities and a reference for educational improvement.

The stories and accompanying names told in this book are fictitious, but are based on the real situations of some schools in the U.S.

CHAPTER I

The Overarching Framework Enveloping this Study

The School as an Open System

SCOTT (1992, 1998) EXAMINED and categorized three most competing views of organizational systems as rational, natural and open. These three concepts though fairly distinct are somewhat complementary. An open system is also rational and natural, and the school integrates all these elements (Hoy & Miskel, 1996). As a rational system, the school strives to achieve its goals structurally and methodically; as a natural system, it is conceived of social groups (administrators, teachers and students) in interrelationships striving for survival. The open system cycle revolves around "inputs", "transformations", and "outputs". The input phase incorporates human, material and financial resources fed into the school; the transformational phase deals with the internal processes and structures of the school as an organization; whereas the output section involves performance outcome measures, the products or the goals (Hoy & Miskel, 1996). For Mouzelis (1967), an open system is a social system with various subsystems embedded in the wider society. An open system is, "a set of interacting elements that acquires inputs from the outside, transforms them, and produces outputs for the environment" (Hoy & Miskel, 1996, p. 26). As an open social organizational system the school incorporates interacting elements, which could be human and material, quantitative and qualitative (see Figure 1).

In this study, the author will be examining the relationships amongst the school climate as openness and health, pupil control ideology, and their interrelationship to effectiveness. Climate in its various forms involves internal processes and structures of the school as an open system. Effectiveness is a performance outcome criterion, it overruns the spheres of the school's input, transformation, and output; hence, it is an integrative open system's measuring instrument.

Socioeconomic status is the grading of an individual or a family in terms of possession and influence over wealth, power and social status; it incorporates parental income, education and occupation. Individual student come to school either with the advantages or burdens associated with socioeconomic status. Giving the right resources of an open and healthy climate the school can transform the human input it receives from its environment into successful people, notwithstanding the low socioeconomic background and the academic burden each student brings.

The family as an open system

The family falls within the confines of the general system theory, a wider base for models of family relationships (Fawcett, 1976). The concept of the open family system had preoccupied family studies for years (Constantine, 1983). As an open system, the family is made up of interrelated parts with members working together within a given environment. As earlier stated, an open system is embedded within an environment; it receives input, processes it and generates output to the same environment (see Figure 1). According to Constantine, "An open system is one which has significant exchanges of matter and/or energy with its environment" (1983, p. 726). An open system is transformational and therefore, non-static. Open systems have boundaries, which could be flexible and dynamic. As a rational system, it is structured; and as a natural system, it is composed of members in interrelationships. The family possesses all these characteristics. However, irrespective of shared commonality in openness among all families, there is no rigid behavioral or operational uniformity among them, "they differ markedly in their manifest patterns of behavior and in the mechanisms by which these patterns are maintained and regulated" (Constantine, 1983, p. 726).

Figure 1
The School and the Family as open system

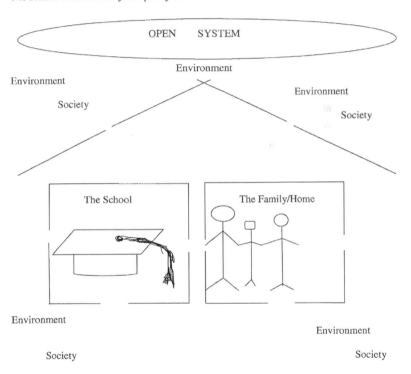

Socioeconomic status incorporates parental income, education, and occupation; it is the grading of an individual or a family in terms of possession and influence over wealth, power and social status. Children enter school with academic strengths and liabilities acquired from their families. The family climate makes up a significant portion of the home environment. A healthy open family system makes a good home, a necessary capital needed by a child to succeed both in the school and the society. The importance of the home in the academic development of a child and his or her later success in the life is of paramount importance. An open functional family with a healthy academic home environment will enhance the academic potentials of a child; a closed dysfunctional family will have an opposite effect.

Open system is therefore, most suitable for the conceptual underpinning guiding the course of this study. The variables to be investigated fall within its confines. The framework of an open system is thus, the conceptual underpinning and the overarching structure shadowing this study. It will be wonderful for the reader to have this in mind as the author explores alternate means of school effectiveness and students academic achievement as bypass to socioeconomic status.

School Climates As Openness, Health And Pupil Control Ideology; And Effectiveness: Definition

When people talk about climate, the tendency is for them to think in terms of the weather conditions: temperature, humidity, rain, sunshine, winds, clouds or the prevailing weather condition of a place. With regard to its usage in school as an organizational concept, there is some similarity but there is contextual difference. It is a technical term for describing the atmospheric condition of the school organizational environment; even in this context, it has many model usages.

The word climate as an organizational term originated from social and industrial psychology and had been in use in those disciplines as a measuring instrument over the years (Pace & Stern, 1958). As a quality of an organization, climate is defined as, "those characteristics that distinguish the organization from other organizations and that influence the behavior of people in the organizations" (Gilmer, 1966, p. 57). Halpin and Croft (1963) borrowing from Parsons and Shils (1967) introduced the element of "personality" into the climate discussion; such that climate is to the organization what personality is to the individual (Hoy & Sabo, 1998). Litwin and Stringer (1968) added perceptual attribute to the discuss and so defined climate as, "a set of measurable properties of the work environment, based on the collective perception of the people who live and work in the environment and demonstrated to influence their behavior" (1968, p. 1). The saying goes that "perception is reality". As a perceptual concept, climate is described as the collective perception of organizational members, which arises from their routine practices, and reversely influences their behaviors and attitudes (Hoy & Miskel, 1996; Hoy & Sabo, 1998).

Climate offers a clear concept to describe the atmosphere or the feel of the school as an organization (Halpin & Croft, 1963). It was described as those characteristics that distinguish one school from another, that influence the behaviors of its members, and give the school its personality (Forehand & Gilmer, 1964; Tagiuri, 1968). Hence, as personality is to the individual so is climate to the school. School climate is a distinctive quality of school environment (Cheng, 1991; Stewart, 1979). Hoy and Miskel constitutively defined school climate as, "a relatively enduring quality of the school environment that is experienced by participants, affects their behavior, and is based on their collective perceptions of behavior in schools" (1996, p. 141). The human and material resources fed into the school affect its activity and productivity; these in turn influence the perception of the principal, teachers and students, which further affect their behaviors.

Climate as openness and health was operationally measured with the Organizational Climate Index (OCI), an instrument developed by Hoy and Sabo (1998). It is a 30-item climatic index derived from Organizational Climate Descriptive Questionnaire (which tests for school openness) and Organizational Health Inventory (which tests for school health).

Pupil control another element of the school (social) climate has been an important concept to both researchers and literatures over the years (Waller, 1932; Silberman, 1970). Willower and Jones (1963) found this concept most fitting for describing the social behaviors of the general public school climate. Their observations and interviews in a junior high school over a period of fourteen months yielded "pupil control" as a dominant motif in 'teacher-student' interaction and 'teacher-teacher' discussion; this also overflows into teacher-principal relationship. Pupil control is therefore, theoretically useful for an integrative understanding of the interrelationships among teachers, students, and administrators (Hoy, 1967). Pupil control ideology is concerned with the social belief aspect of the school culture or environment; it is the central motive or ideology from which students are viewed, and a dominant guide to their control.

There are two perspectives to climate in this study: climate as openness and health (condensed into organizational climate index OCI) and climate as pupil control ideology (PCI). These climatic indexes

(OCI and PCI) will be used as predictor or independent variables in this study.

Effectiveness is very significant concept to open organizational systems, although it is known to be very elusive (Cameron & Whetten, 1983). There is no agreement on how the concept of effectiveness is to be defined or conceptualized among scholars, but, it still continues to be crucial, because of its theoretical, empirical, and practical importance. Efforts have been made toward the study of school effectiveness, but were limited on conceptual and theoretical grounds. Hoy and Ferguson, citing Georgopoulos and Tannenbaum (1957) defined effectiveness as, " 'the extent to which any organization as a social system, given certain resources and means, fulfills its objectives without incapacitating its means and resources and without placing undue strain upon its members' " (1985, p. 121). This definition is quite in line with the subjective model offered by Paul Mott who defined organizational effectiveness as "the ability of an organization to mobilize its centers of power for action – production and adaptation" (1972, p. 17). Mott's model integrates the characteristics of the two opposing organizational concepts (the system resource and the goal models), giving his model a performance-outcome orientation or a process-result characteristic. Hence the effectiveness of a school is not just based on the results (output) but on the efficiency of its operation (transformation or process). The school effectiveness will be measured with the Index of Perceived Organizational Effectiveness (IPOE), an 8-item index originally developed by Mott (1972), and modified by Miskel, McDonald and Bloom (1983) for use in schools; it is the dependent variable in this study.

CHAPTER II

The Historical Development of the Concepts: School Climate and School Effectiveness

School Climate

As PREVIOUSLY STATED, CLIMATE as used in this study is a combination of openness and health, and pupil control ideology. The following historical narratives are necessary as explicative guide to the theoretical development of school's openness and health, and pupil control ideology. These narratives will lead to a point where openness and health were merged into four simple factors of the school organizational climate index (OCI). Further description will explain the historical origin of pupil control ideology (PCI).

The goal of studying climate is to demonstrate its importance as a personality of a school. As one's personality is vital for the person's survival, development and growth so also is school climate. Climate is presented here as the means and end of school improvement and change, as that which offers a better alternative to socioeconomic status which is not so pliable or changeable. Low socioeconomic status has remained a hindering factor to the academic achievement of children and their future success in adult life. By this study, this author attempts to proffer solution, rather than present a list of problems.

What Does It Mean For a School To Be Open or Closed?

Halpin and Croft (1963) were the first to conceptualize and measure the organizational climate of the school. These authors made a study of the climate of seventy-one elementary schools involving 1151 teachers. Influenced by Rokeach (1960), these aforementioned authors conceptualized elementary school climate along an open-closed continuum precipitating "Organizational Climate Descriptive Questionnaire" (OCDQ). The distinctive feature of an open school climate is the degree of its authenticity; both the principal and the faculty are genuine. Closed school climate is the antithesis of open school climate. In a closed school climate, the behaviors of the principal and teachers are inauthentic.

The above seminal work, though useful for some time, had weaknesses and limitations (Andrews, 1965; Silver, 1983). The OCDQ instrument was also inadequate for the measurement of the middle and secondary school climates. Having outlived its reliability with the passage of time there was an undertaking to revise the OCDQ by Hoy and Clover (1986); other researchers also followed such as, Hoy, Hoffman, Sabo, and Bliss (1996).

In a series of exploratory factor analyses, involving thirty-eight schools, Hoy and Clover's (1986) revised the OCDQ, changing the name to Revised Organizational Climate Descriptive Questionnaire for Elementary Schools (OCDQ-RE). This is a 42-item instrument with six subtests describing principal-teacher and teacher-teacher behaviors. The alpha coefficient of reliabilities ranged from .75 to .95. The six dimensions have strong construct validity and factor stability. The instrument measures three aspects of "principal behavior" and three of "teacher behavior". The dimensions (subtests) for the principal behavior were *supportive principal behavior, directive principal behavior,* and *restrictive principal behavior.* Supportive principal behavior is that which is open to teachers' suggestions, which respect the competence of teachers with interest in their personal and professional welfare. Directive principal behavior is the principal behavior that is rigid, with closed monitoring and control over teachers' activities. Restrictive principal behaviors are those principal behaviors that hinder rather than facilitate the work of teachers, with teachers perceiving the principal as burdening them with unnecessary demands.

Hoy and Clover (1986), presented the principal-teacher relationships along an open-closed continuum. Open principal behavior is marked by enabling environment in which the effort of teachers are genuinely supported. The principal encourages teachers' participation and contribution, freeing them from unnecessary busywork so that they can concentrate on the task of teaching and learning. Open principal behavior is genuine and authentic. On the other hand, closed principal behavior (the antithesis of open principal behavior) is rigid, controlling and unsupportive; it is the principal behavior that is closed and inauthentic. The OCDQ-RE also measures three aspects of teacher behavior, which are *collegial teacher behavior, intimate teacher behavior,* and *disengaged teacher behavior.* Collegial teacher behavior leads to open and professional interactions among teachers, with teachers exhibiting pride in their school as they mutually accept and respect each other's competence. Disengaged teacher behavior is that unprofessional attitudes among teachers, when teachers have no common goal and their efforts are unproductive. Intimate teacher behavior leads to cohesive and strong social bond among teachers who exhibit friendliness and support for one another. Like principal behavior, teacher-teacher relationships were also conceptualized along an open-closed continuum. Teacher behavior is open when it is sincere, positive and supportive; with teachers being warm, friendly, respectful and tolerant of each other. To be precise, open teacher behavior is authentic. Closed teacher behavior is the antithesis of open teacher behavior; teachers are loathsome, divisive, apathetic, unsupportive and intolerant of one another. Closed teacher behavior is inauthentic.

As already stated, the OCDQ-RE measures two general factors, which are, openness or closedness of principal behavior, and openness or closedness of teacher behavior. From these factors, Hoy and Clover (1986) developed a school climate typology of four climatic prototypes, which are *open climate, engaged climate, disengaged climate, and closed climate.* A congruence of openness in which the principal and teacher behaviors are open, leads to "open school climate." If both sets of behaviors are closed, the result is "closed school climate." On the other hand, there are incongruent behavior patterns. The principal leadership might be open with the teachers but if the teachers are closed with the principal and each other; this pattern is called "disengaged school climate." However, if the principal is closed with the teachers, and the teachers are open with each other; the result is "engaged school climate" (Hoy, Tarter & Kottkamp, 1991) (see Figure 2).

Figure 2
Typology of elementary school climate (Hoy and Clover, 1986)

<table>
<tr><td></td><td></td><td colspan="2" align="center">PRINCIPAL BEHAVIOR</td></tr>
<tr><td></td><td></td><td align="center">Open</td><td align="center">Closed</td></tr>
<tr><td></td><td>Open</td><td align="center">Open
Climate</td><td align="center">Engaged
Climate</td></tr>
<tr><td>TEACHER BEHAVIOR</td><td></td><td></td><td></td></tr>
<tr><td></td><td>Close</td><td align="center">Disengaged
Climate</td><td align="center">Closed
Climate</td></tr>
</table>

Table 1
Schools Climate: Items, Dimensions, Factors and Typologies

		Elementary School Climate	*Middle School Climate*	*Secondary School Climate*
Items Number		42	50	34
Climate	Dimensions/Subtests	1. Supportive Principal Behavior 2. Directive Principal Behavior 3. Restrictive Principal Behavior 4. Collegial Teacher Behavior 5. Intimate Teacher Behavior 6. Disengaged Teacher Behavior	1. Supportive Principal Behavior 2. Directive Principal Behavior 3. Restrictive Principal Behavior 4. Collegial Teacher Behavior 5. Committed Teacher Behavior 6. Disengaged Teacher Behavior	1. Supportive Principal Behavior 2. Directive Principal Behavior 3. Engaged Teacher Behavior 4. Frustrated Teacher Behavior 5. Intimate Teacher Behavior
General Factors		1. Openness in Faculty Relations 2. Closedness in Principal Leadership	1.Openness in Principal Behavior 2. Openness in Teacher Behavior	1.Openness in Principal/Teacher Behavior 2. Intimacy
Climate Typology		Open Climate Engaged Climate Disengaged Climate Closed Climate	Open Climate Engaged Climate Disengaged Climate Closed Climate	Open Climate Closed Climate

11

The Organizational Climate Descriptive Questionnaire (OCDQ-RM), an instrument for measuring middle school climate was developed by Hoy, Hoffman, Sabo, and Bliss (1996). It has fifty items and six dimensions, which are *supportive principal behavior, directive principal behavior, restrictive principal behavior, collegial teacher behavior, committed teacher behavior* and *disengaged teacher behavior.* The secondary school climate (OCDQ-RS) instrument was developed by Kottkamp, Mulhern, and Hoy (1987) with seventy-eight schools in New Jersey; it had thirty-four items and five dimensions. These dimensions are *supportive principal behavior, directive principal behavior, engaged teacher behavior, frustrated teacher behavior,* and *intimate teacher behavior* (see Table 1).

Besides viewing school climate along an open closed continuum, schools could also be described as healthy or unhealthy. The school organizational health climate metaphor describes the interactive dynamics of the professional relationship among students, teachers, and administrators (Hoy & Sabo, 1998).

What Does It Mean For a School To Be Healthy or Unhealthy?

When people talk about "health" as it relates to a human being they tend to think in terms of a person's state of physical, mental, and social well-being. The absence of illness in one's body, mind and spirit is often associated with good health. However, there is contextual difference regarding its usage in the school as an organization.

The explicit use of the health metaphor as it pertains to an organization appeared first in the work of Miles (1965) for the analysis of schools' organizational health. Miles defined a healthy organization as one that "not only survives in its environment, but continues to cope adequately over the long haul, and continuously develops and extends its surviving and coping abilities" (1969, p. 378). Environmental survival and coping abilities are ongoing processes for the health of any organization, which may be effective and ineffective from day to day but in the long run evades continuous ineffectiveness (Hoy, Tarter & Kottkamp, 1991).

Hoy and Feldman (1987) were the first to develop a more reliable theoretical measure of the concept of organizational health in schools by turning their attention to the theoretical analyses of Parsons, Bales, and Shils (1953), and that of Etzioni (1975). Parsons and colleagues postulated that social systems must solve four basic problems in order to survive, grow, and develop, which are, adaptation, goal attainment, integration, and latency (Parsons et al., 1953). In other words, social systems must accommodate to their environments, set and implement their goals, preserve cohesive systems, and create and maintain unique values (Hoy, Hannum, & Tschannen-Moran, 1998). Therefore, in order to survive, grow, and be effective, healthy schools must, "adapt to their environments, achieve their goals, and infuse common values and solidarity into the teacher work group" (Hoy & Sabo, 1998, p. 55). "Adaptation and goal achievement" were categorized as *instrumental needs,* whereas "integration and latency" were the mark of *expressive needs* (Parsons, 1967). A school that cannot adapt or achieve its goals looses its reason for existence, whereas a school that cannot integrate its members loses them.

Citing the work of Parsons, Bales, and Shils (1953), Hoy and Feldman (1987) postulated that schools must have three levels of control over the above needs, which are, *the technical, the managerial,* and *the institutional levels of control.* The technical level is concerned with teaching and learning; the managerial is known for internal administrative function of the school; the institutional level connects the school with its environment. The levels of control patterns enumerated above offer theoretical foundation for the definition and operationalization of the organizational health of a school. Consequently, a healthy school is, "one in which the technical, managerial, and institutional levels are in harmony; and the school is meeting both its instrumental and expressive needs as it successfully copes with disruptive external forces and directs its energies toward its mission" (Hoy & Feldman, p. 31).

Hoy and Feldman conceptualized and measured the OHI of seventy-eight secondary schools; this produced forty-four items with seven dimensions, and has alpha coefficient of reliabilities that ranged from .87 to .95. The dimensional elements of OHI are *institutional integrity, principal influence, consideration, initiating structure, resource support, morale,* and *academic emphasis. Institutional integrity* is the ability of a school to cope with its environment, in which teachers are protected from unreasonable demands from the parents and the community. *Principal influence* is the principal's ability to influence the superiors without hindrance. In *Consideration,* the principal is friendly, approachable and interested in the personal welfares of the teachers.

With *Initiating structure,* the principal is task and achievement oriented. *Resource support* is when teachers receive necessary instructional supplies, with extra materials still available upon their request. *Morale* is teachers' friendliness, openness, enthusiasm, and trust amongst themselves. In *academic emphasis*, teachers set high but achievable academic goals and students work hard to achieve those goals and respect those who get good grades, in an orderly but serious learning environment.

When compared with the Parsons' level of control, 'institutional integrity' relates to the institutional level; 'principal influence', 'consideration', 'initiating structure', and 'resource support' concerns the managerial level, whereas 'morale' and 'academic emphasis' belong to the technical level (Hoy, Tarter & Kottkamp, 1991) (see Table 2).

Hoy and Feldman (1987) further performed a second order factor analysis, which resulted in a strong general factor accounting for 45% of the variance. This factor identified schools, which are relatively strong on the entire seven dimensions; the factor was called "School health". The authors determined an index of school health by adding the standard scores of the seven subtests; the higher the score, the healthier the school. A model of a healthy and unhealthy school was then determined along a continuum ranging from healthy to unhealthy. In a healthy school there is high institutional integrity, principal influence, consideration, initiating structure, resource support, morale, and academic emphasis (a healthy school is high in all the seven dimensions); an unhealthy school is low in all the dimensions. In a healthy school, the technical, the managerial, and the institutional levels are in harmony; the school is meeting both its instrumental and expressive needs, and successfully coping with disruptive external forces as it directs its energy toward its mission. Harmony and cooperation in all the levels are the hallmarks of a healthy school (Etzioni, 1975; Nadler & Tushman, 1989). An unhealthy school is the opposite; there is no harmony and cooperation in the technical, managerial and institutional levels.

From the aforementioned one can say that school climate as health has all the elements to turn a failing school around notwithstanding the low socioeconomic background of the students. *With institutional integrity* the school has the ability to cope with its environment, in which teachers are protected from unreasonable demands from the parents and the community, such that only reasonable demands are heeded to; with *principal influence*, the principal has the ability to influence superiors without hindrance, he or she is a goal-getter for the school; with *consideration*, the principal is friendly with teachers, approachable and interested in the personal welfares of the teachers, this helps the teachers to give their best in teaching; with *initiating structure*, the principal is task and achievement oriented, bearing in mind that academic achievement is the goal of teaching and learning; with *resource support* teachers receive necessary instructional supplies, with extra materials still available upon their request, so that they can focus on the task of teaching and learning; with *morale* teachers are friendly, open, enthusiastic, and trustworthy, this comrade feeling among teachers builds social cohesiveness and helps them identify with the school; with *academic emphasis*, teachers set high but achievable academic goals and students work hard to achieve those goals and respect those who get good grades, when the learning environment is orderly and serious; the objective of schooling is realized when students are working hard and achieving their academic goals. A school that has all these qualities is a healthy school. These among others set climate as health apart as a means for improving a failing school or a means to turn a low performing school around into a high performing one.

Hoy, Tarter and Kottkamp (1991) were the first to develop the organizational health inventory for elementary school (OHI-E). With a sample of seventy-eight schools, the researchers formed the OHI-E, which has thirty-seven items and five dimensions. The dimensions are *teacher affiliation, collegial leadership, resource influence, institutional integrity,* and *academic emphasis.* Building on the work of Hoy and colleagues (1987; 1991), Hoy and Sabo (1998) developed the middle school organizational health index (OHI-M) from that of both the secondary and the elementary schools' inventories outlined above. This work involved eighty-six middle schools in New Jersey and has high factor stability; the dimensions are *academic emphasis, teacher affiliation, collegial leadership, principal influence, resource support,* and *institutional integrity* (see Table 3).

Table 2

Health Dimensions, Functions, Activity, and Levels

Levels and Health Dimension	Function	Activity
INSTITUTIONAL LEVEL Institutional Integrity	Adaptation	Instrumental
MANAGERIAL LEVEL Principal Influence Consideration	Integration and Latency Integration and Latency	Expressive Expressive
Initiating Structure Resource Support	Goal Achievement Adaptation	Instrumental Instrumental
TECHNICAL LEVEL Academic Emphasis Morale	Goal Achievement Integration and Latency	Instrumental Expressive

Table 3

Schools Health Climate, Items, Dimensions, Factors and Typologies

	Elementary School Health	Middle School Health	Secondary School Health
Number of Items	37	45	44
Dimensions	1. Teacher Affiliation 2. Collegial Leadership 3. Resource Influence 4 Institutional Integrity 5. Academic Emphasis	1.Academic Emphasis 2. Teacher Affiliation 3. Collegial Leadership 4. Principal Influence 5. Resource Support 6.Institutional Integrity	1.Institutional Integrity 2. Principal Influence 3. Consideration 4. Initiating Structure 5. Resource Support 6. Moral 7.Academic Emphasis
Climate Typology	Healthy School Unhealthy School	Healthy School Unhealthy School	Healthy School Unhealthy School

An Open School Is Also a Healthy School

William and Travon are friends; both attend a public school in the Southeastern part of the U.S. The school is composed of 66 percent African Americans, 15 percent Whites, 13 percent Latinos, 5.5 percent Asians and 0.5 percent Native American. Students in this public school are mainly low income with 87 percent eligible for free or reduced-price lunch.

Seven years ago, student achievement in this school district was low, with the school placed bellow the state average in math and reading; most students scored in the bottom quartile of the state assessment. Two years later, the state worked out a new contract with the teachers and took over the district public schools; the school board was changed, superintendent resigned, curriculum and textbooks were changed, new and competent principals and teachers were hired, teacher professional development was made more effective, there was integrative and effective parent involvement, and class sizes were reduced. There is now more extracurricular and after school intellectual stimulating programs.

William and his friend Travon can now boast of a school that has risen from an underperforming to a high performing school. The district received a five year grant from a science foundation to make improvements in science and mathematics. The principal has administrative experience and is willing to work around the rules to hire and keep qualified teachers; she is an instructional leader and is more visible, involved and supportive of teachers' professional development. Teachers are experienced and have higher expectation of their students. They believe that every student can learn and go beyond their contract duties in taking responsibilities for their students' learning; they spend more time teaching mathematics, reading and science. Teachers are committed to this school, they have 95 percent attendance rate and feel responsible for their students' achievement and behaviors. Teacher work in collegiality with each other and with the principal; there is a high morale and team spirit among the teaching force. The school has clear and effective disciplinary policy that is oriented to the goal of teaching and learning.

William and his friend are motivated to learn, there is healthy competition among the student population. William and Travon know the expectation of their teacher and their parents and are all hoping to go to college. Their teacher is in continual communication with their parents about their progress in class and areas they need to improve. There is a healthy parent school relationship. Parents are welcome to the school anytime; they only have to check in at the office. Parents volunteer at the school and the principal and teachers are responsive to parents. The school has parent outreach program and parent homework help line for parents who are finding it difficult to help their children with their homework. Through parent training the school helps parents on the skills they need to partner with the school. Parents are sometimes invited to their child's classrooms to talk about their careers and jobs. They are encouraged to donate age appropriate books to their children's classrooms and to borrow books from the school to read for their children. The principal knows the neighborhood and is well known and respected in the community.

This is a typical school that has risen from being closed and unhealthy to an open and healthy school.

The climate metaphors of openness and health had for a long time captured the attention of scholars and practitioners in the analyses of school organizational environment as earlier reviewed. School Openness and health have empirical relationships and they overlap in various characteristics. Open schools tend to be healthy and healthy schools are often times open (Hoy, Tarter & Kottkamp, 1991). Giving this compatibility, Hoy and Sabo (1998) integrated both measures into a simple but comprehensive measure of school climate. With the middle school openness and health (OCDQ-RM), the authors performed a second-order principal analysis involving the six dimensions and twelve factors of openness and health (see Table 1 & 3). They also performed an analysis that resulted in a reduction of both climate dimensions from twelve factors to four; it has only thirty items. They called this measure, organizational climate index (OCI). The validity and reliability of this measuring instrument was confirmed in a correlation and regression analyses with students' achievement in Math, Reading, and Writing, and also in a regression analysis with overall school effectiveness.

Factor I contained four variables, which are *supportive principal behavior, collegial leadership, directive principal behavior* and *restrictive principal behavior.* Supportive principal behavior and collegial leadership loaded strongly in the positive direction, whereas directive principal behavior and restrictive principal behavior loaded strongly in the negative direction. **Factor I was then called *collegial leadership* because it describes the relationship between the principal and the teachers; it is principal's behavior that is open and supportive, but nondirective or restrictive (Hoy & Sabo, 1998).**

Factor II contained four variables, which are *teacher commitment, teacher collegiality, teacher affiliation and teacher disengagement.* Teacher commitment, teacher collegiality and teacher affiliation loaded in the positive direction, whereas teacher disengagement loaded negatively. **Factor II was therefore called** *teacher professionalism,* **which indicates the relationships among teachers. This factor was defined as teachers' committed behavior to their students, their acquaintance with the teaching task, their respect, warmth and friendliness among their colleagues.**

Factor III has *academic emphasis, resource support,* and *principal influence.* This factor was named *academic press.* **It described the setting of high but achievable academic goals by teachers on the one hand and the positive response to those challenges by students on the other, complemented by the principal's influence with the superiors in supplying needed resources.**

Factor IV was a one positive variable, it contained *institutional integrity;* **this factor was then called** *environmental press.* Factor four is indicative of inside academic press and outside environmental press; it also controls for possible mislabeling as alarmed by previous researchers (Hoy, Tarter & Kottkamp, 1991). **Factor IV signifies a strong pressure from parents and community to influence and change school policy and function (Hoy & Sabo, 1998), complemented by internal press from the principal and teachers to improve schooling.**

These four dimensions of climate (factors I, II, III, and IV) articulate prudently the essence of an open school and a healthy school. Hoy and Sabo (1998) further examined these four factors in the light of the Parsons' (1953) framework according to the three organizational levels, which are "the institutional, the managerial, and the technical levels." Environmental press corresponds to the institutional level, collegial leadership to the managerial level, whereas teacher professionalism and academic press belong to the technical level. These according to Hoy and Sabo match up to four important school linkages: *community-school* linkage (environmental press), *principal-teacher* linkage (collegial leadership), *teacher-teacher* linkage (teacher professionalism), and *teacher-student* linkage (academic press) (see table 4). These are all the actors and factors needed by any school to improve, succeed and progress.

The Organizational Climate Index (OCI) is indeed comprehensive, in that it was developed from the middle school's openness and health dimensions, which were respectively created from the elementary and the secondary schools' openness and health dimensions.

As earlier stated, the reason for the investigation of school climate is to explore its richness as an alternative to socioeconomic status, as a means and end of school improvement and as a condition for academic achievement of students who are carrying the burden of low socioeconomic status. An open and healthy school climate seems to have all the ingredients for school improvement and students' academic achievement. Climate is described as the personality of the school. Just as one's personality is significant for one's survival, growth and development so is climate to the school.

In an open and healthy school climate, teachers like and respect their colleagues; they are committed to their students and their teaching task (there is, high *teacher professionalism*); the principal is viewed as an ally in improving instruction, he or she is open, friendly, respectful, and supportive of the teachers, without sacrificing high standards of performance; the principal is also nonrestrictive, and teachers cooperate freely with the principal (there is, strong *collegial leadership*). An open and healthy school climate is known by internal press for academic achievement; teachers set high but achievable academic goals, and students work hard to achieve those goals and respect those who get good grades; instructional materials are available upon request from the principal, whom the teachers perceive as influential with the superiors (there is high *academic emphasis*). An open and healthy school climate is also marked by reasonable external press from the parents and the community, complemented by internal press from the faculty to improve schooling (there is, high *environmental press*).

School climate is a pervasive concept. Although a school can be described as open or closed, healthy or unhealthy, there is another climatic type that describes the social behaviors of the general public school climate, a dominant motif in teacher-student interaction and teacher-teacher discussion; this can describe a school as either humanistic or custodial.

Table 4
Organizational Climate Factors, Perspectives and Linkages

LINKAGES	LEVELS OF CONTROL		
	Technical Level	*Managerial Level*	*Institutional Level*
Community-School			Environmental Press
Principal-Teacher		Collegial Leadership	
Teacher-Teacher	Teacher Professionalism		
Teacher-Student	Academic Press		

Figure 3
Custodialism - Humanism Continuum

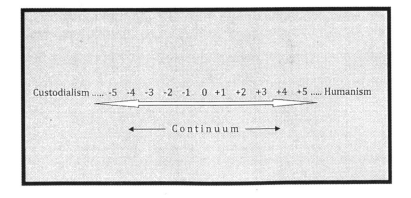

What Does It Mean For a School Ideology
to Be Humanistic or Custodial

Otunba is a 9 year old black male student in a third-grade class in a public school located in a poor neighborhood in the Midwestern part of the U.S. Not too long ago, his family migrated to the U.S from a country in West Africa, having won the U.S. Visa Lottery. He has a little sister who attends the same public school with him, within their neighborhood. The school's ethnic compositions are 70 percent Blacks, 10 percent Latinos, 8 percent Whites and 12 percent Asians. His father who was an auto mechanic in his West African country now works as a night watchman at an auto dealing company where he makes some money to support his family, and hopes to train to be a car mechanic after his wife finishes school. His mother, who was a midwife in her country in West Africa, cannot use her certificate here in the U.S to get a job, she now works as a house cleaner at the local mall in the day and is training to be a registered nurse in the evening at the community college. They speak their country's English but are perceived as having a heavy ascent by their neighbors. Otunba has difficulty communicating in school; he has no friend, other kids make fun of him and laugh at his ascent. His teacher said he has a funny name and has tried to change it but his parents objected. Otunba's school has a high student teacher ratio and large class sizes with less individual attention for each student. There are fewer extracurricular activities, few school nurses and social workers. The school building and the school play ground are poorly maintained. The classrooms have poorly maintained infrastructures; the school environment is less motivating for learning; the school is failing, standardized test scores are below par. Teachers have low morale and often complain that most of their students are disruptive in class that a few others have behavioral problems and that parents are uncooperative. The principal rarely visits the classrooms; teachers also complain of not being supported by the principal, who is either busy in his office most of the time or is out of the school building for one school problem or the other. For these teachers, the classroom is warfare and teaching is hassle. Since going for work is matter of survival as perceived by these teachers, they have devised a way to control the external threat posed by their students whom they perceive as trouble makers to be controlled by sanctions and punishment. These teachers have a custodial pupil control ideology towards their students, and this is a typical school where humanistic ideology is lacking.

The attitudes and behaviors of educators especially those of teachers are often influenced by social and psychological factors surrounding them (Hoy, 2001). The in-group, out-group dichotomy often comes into play in the natural inclination of these educators to adopt a stance in controlling external threats from their students, the out-group (Sherif, 1961). *Pupil control* has been an important concept to both researchers and literatures over the years (Waller, 1932; Silberman, 1970). Willower and Jones (1963) found this concept most fitting for describing the social behaviors of the general public school climate. These authors made an observation and interview in a junior high school over a period of fourteen months; their study yielded "pupil control" as a dominant motif in teacher-student interaction and teacher-teacher discussion, which also overflows into teacher-principal relationship. Pupil control is therefore, theoretically useful not only for research but also for an integrative understanding of the interrelationships among teachers, students, and administrators (Hoy, 1967). It is concerned with the social belief aspect of the school climate. Pupil control is the central motive or ideology from which students are viewed and a dominant guide to their control.

Borrowing from Gilbert and Levinson (1957), Willower, Eidell and Hoy (1967) defined and developed pupil control ideology initially as a concept and then as a measuring instrument for studies on schools. Gilbert and Levinson had earlier made a study of the structure and staff ideology of patients' control in a public mental hospital (a total institution). Knowing that that client selection and participation was mandatory in mental hospitals, staff ideology of patients' control was operationalized and measured in a continuum with polarities ranging from *custodialism* to *humanism* (see Figure 3). Custodialism signifies rigid viewpoints and policies of the mental hospital; whereas humanism denotes the conception of the hospital as a community of citizens with a wide range of human needs to be met.

Willower, Eidell, and Hoy (1967) adapted the above mentioned framework to a public school, a service organization and a partial institution. They noted that custodial ideology is characterized by pessimism and watchful mistrust of students, viewed as irresponsible and undisciplined people to be controlled with sanctions and punishments.

In this context, students' behaviors are judged moralistically. The model for this ideology they contend is a school in which behaviors are rigidly and tightly controlled and maintenance of order given priority. In custodial schools, the stress on control is generally external; there is a pessimistic view of students (Willower, 1965). Humanism, in contrast, is characterized by trustfulness, and the understanding and acceptance of students as people who can freely learn and accept responsibilities for their behaviors. The model for humanism is a learning community in which interpersonal behaviors are warm and friendly. Behaviors are interpreted psychologically and socially rather than judgmentally (Nachtscheim & Hoy, 1976). Humanistic schools have an optimistic view of students; emphasis is placed on internal control of students rather than external.

The measuring form for pupil control ideology (PCI) was developed by Willower, Eidell, and Hoy (1967), for the measurement of the PCI of professional staff members of public schools. This is a 20-item Likert-type scale designed to tap custodial and humanistic framework, with items scored and summed up, such that the higher the score, the more custodial the school orientation. Negative significant custodialism inversely means positive significant humanism. This instrument measures ideology not behavior. The aforementioned authors supported the validity of this instrument by comparing it with the principals' independent assessment of the pupil control ideology of teachers. Further validation was determined by comparing schools known to be reputably humanistic, with others. The instrument has split-half reliabilities coefficient ranging from .91 to .95.

Public schools are service organization in which client participation is mandatory. Teachers have no choice over students' selection, making pupil control ideology a central issue in teacher-teacher interaction and teacher-student relationship (Hoy & Henderson, 1983). The pupil control typology (PCI) has been useful over the years for the study of modes of thought guiding professional policies, adaptations, and behaviors in schools (Denig, 1999; Hall, Hall, & Abaci, 1997; Nachtscheim & Hoy, 1976). The PCI is another perspective of school's climate besides climate as OCI (Schmidt & Jacobson, 1990). The PCI measures school social climate.

As earlier stated, the reason for the investigation of school climate is to explore its richness as an alternative to low socioeconomic status, a predetermined burden carried by most low achieving students. Open and healthy school climate is the means and end of schools' survival, development and growth; I will explore its implications for school effectiveness and thereafter student achievement. Humanistic school climate is characterized by trustfulness, and the understanding and acceptance of students as people who can freely learn and accept responsibilities for their behaviors; this is typified by a learning community in which interpersonal behaviors are warm and friendly. Humanistic schools have optimistic views of students; teachers in such schools believe their students can freely learn. By challenging why pupils' failures and future statuses in life are not destined on their parents' incomes, educational attainments and neighborhoods, this author is seeking to recommend climate as alternative routes to academic achievement as a bypass to socioeconomic status. The author is seeking to do this through a research study done in New York City public schools, an area with low socioeconomic status. In this study, the strength, richness and validity of climate variables was measured with the criterion of effectiveness.

Effectiveness as a Better Criterion for Measuring School's Resource, Input, Transformation and Output

As an open system the school receives input from its environment, transforms it and generates output to the same environment. Effectiveness appears to offer a better criterion for measuring these aforesaid elements. Having been described as the apex and abyss of organizational analysis, effectiveness has the ambivalence of being theoretically and practically important but at the same time slippery and elusive (Hoy & Miskel, 1996). There has been close to thirty criterion measures of effectiveness identified by scholars (Campbell, 1977). The concept of effectiveness was so complex that there were difficulties finding the most representative variable or variables to measure it. Many effectiveness studies were criticized on issues of measurement, statistics, methodology and theory (Hoy & Ferguson, 1985). Nevertheless, two opposing camps stand out in this historical attempt toward its description and measurement, and these are "the goal model" and "the system-resource model." For the goal model, "a school is effective if the outcome of its activities meets or exceeds its goals" (Hoy & Miskel, 1996, p. 239). For the system-resource model, an effective organization is determined by, "the internal consistency of the organization, the efficiency of use of its resources, the success of its coping mechanisms, and its ability to compete with others for resources, especially scarce ones" (Hoy & Ferguson, 1985, p. 120). Since, both models are fraught with conceptual and theoretical inadequacies, a synthesis was suggested by scholars like Campbell (1977), Goodman and Pennings (1977), and Steers (1977). Other unsettled issues like time perspective, constituency, and criteria to use for the measure of effectiveness gave support to the need for a more comprehensive measure (Hoy & Miskel, 1996).

Paul Mott (1972) therefore, developed a multi-faceted criterion measurement of organizational effectiveness, which combined both performance and outcome (system resource and goal) characteristics like quantity of the product, quality of the product, efficiency, adaptability, and flexibility. For Mott, effective organizations are those that produce more, have more quality outputs, and adapt more effectively to their internal and external problems. He developed a measuring index known as the "Index of Organizational Effectiveness" (IOE). This index was tested at ten hospitals and the National Aeronautics and Space Administration (NASA) in the US. All the five criteria, which reflected both the ability of the organization to achieve its goals and adapt to its environment were consistent with the goal and system-resource models (Hoy & Miskel, 1996). Mott provided far-reaching indicators of validity for his model. The 8-item index was tested for reliability by comparing the responses of professional groups within an organization and by involving the assessments of external experts. Mott found his instrument in agreement with objective measures.

Miskel, Fevurly and Stewart (1979) adapted Mott's IOE index and applied it to a sample of 114 schools. The independent variables were the school structure, measured with the "Structural Properties Questionnaire" (SPQ), and the school organizational process, measured with the "Profile Of School form 3" (POS). The rest of the independent variables were "Loyalty" and "Job satisfaction." Perceived Organizational Effectiveness (one of the dependent variables) was measured with the "Index of Perceived Organizational Effectiveness" for schools (IPOE), an 8-item index modified for use in schools. It has an alpha coefficient of reliability of .89. As in Mott's study, the school's overall effectiveness was measured along the dimensions of quantity and quality of the product, efficiency, adaptability and flexibility. For Miskel and colleagues, the IPOE proved to be a valid and reliable measure of effectiveness for schools.

Hoy and Ferguson (1985), offered a multidimensional perspective to the organizational effectiveness of schools. Using the Parsons' (1953) framework, they conceived the school as an open and rational system, concerned with process and outcome, viability and goal, in the midst of environmental constraints. Parsons (1953; 1960) postulated that for any organization to develop, survive, and grow, it must solve the basic problems of adaptation, goal attainment, integration, and latency. With these Parsons' dimensions, Hoy and Ferguson developed a multidimensional construct of organizational effectiveness based on the following operational criteria: *innovation, academic achievement, cohesiveness, and organizational commitment.* All the criteria correlated with the expert rating of effectiveness. This subjective index of organizational effectiveness had a strong correlation with expert ratings of effectiveness (r = .75). Though limited in some ways, this comprehensive attempt by Hoy and Ferguson was a robust confirmation of the construct validity and reliability of the Index of Perceived organizational effectiveness (IPOE), used in this study.

Paul Mott's effectiveness instrument is a reliable measure, and has been validated by researchers over the years (Hoy & Ferguson, 1985). Since it is based on open organizational system and process-result characteristics, it will be useful as a dependent variable in this study for determining the significance of climate as the means and end of school product, efficiency, adaptability, and flexibility, and as a consequent of student academic achievement. In order to justify school climate as a better and a more functional alternative to socioeconomic status the author will be employing effectiveness as a reliable and dependable criterion for measuring the significance of climate in schools.

CHAPTER III

Rationale and Propositions

On the Relationship between Open and Healthy School, and School with Humanistic or Custodial Ideology

IN THIS LITERATURE BASED rationale, the author will explain the relationship between the two climate measures used in this study, which are openness and health, and pupil control ideology, to see how they are related and where they differ. These relationships will lead to the prediction of the hypotheses guiding the course of this study. These literature reviews are necessary to establish how previous studies have directly or indirectly demonstrated the relationship between climate elements and also to show the rational for this study.

Climate as openness and pupil control though different in some ways are compatible in other ways (Hoy & Miskel, 1996). Appleberry and Hoy (1969) while using the pupil control ideology (PCI) form, developed by Willower and colleagues (1967) and the organizational climate descriptive questionnaire (OCDQ) created by Halpin and Croft (1963) found strong relationship between humanistic pupil control orientation and openness of elementary school climate (r = - .61, p < .01). Lunenburg (1984) found that schools with custodial ideologies have significantly lower *espirit*, lower *thrust*, and higher *disengagement*. Hoy and Henderson (1983) equally found a positive relationship between openness of school climate and humanistic pupil control orientation.

Surprisingly, Kottkamp and Mulhern (1987) did not find significant relationship between the revised secondary school climate questionnaire (OCDQ-RS) and pupil control ideology. This result they said may be attributed to a number of factors like construct differences in the two instruments and some differences in data collection strategy. Finkelstein (1999), nevertheless, found a positive correlation between school health and pupil control ideology (r = -.38, p < .05). Given the theoretical foundations of organizational climate index (OCI) factors, its psychometric powers and its pervasiveness, this author is predicting a positive relationship between organizational climate (OCI) and humanistic pupil control ideology.

Collegial leadership, a dimension of organizational climate index (openness and health), describes the principal's behavior that is open and supportive but nonrestrictive and directive; in other words, authentic principal's behavior (Halpin & Croft, 1963). Hoy and Henderson (1983) in a study involving 591 teachers in 42 elementary schools in New Jersey found significant relationships among principal authenticity, openness of school climate, and pupil control orientation. Openness correlated with the humanistic pupil control of the school (r = .63, p < .01; r = -.44, p < .01). Principal's authenticity is the leader's behavior as perceived by the teachers. Pupil control is more of teacher-teacher and teacher-student interaction than of principal-teacher relationship. Principal's interaction with students is merely indirect and mainly through the mediation of teachers. Nevertheless, since collegial leadership defines an open and authentic principal's behavior with the teachers; it is projected that principal's openness and supportiveness of teachers should lead to more humanistic teachers' behaviors towards the students. Therefore, it is expected in this study that there will be a positive relationship between collegial leadership and humanistic pupil control ideology.

Teacher professionalism, another organizational climate index factor, defines teacher friendliness and respect for colleagues, and teacher commitment to the students and the teaching task (Hoy, Hannum & Tschannen-Moran, 1998). Hoy and Miskel (1996) said that pupil control ideology is more a property of teacher-student interaction than of principal behavior, because, teachers are more directly involved with pupil control than the principal. Willower and Landis (1970) associated professional orientation of teachers with humanistic ideology. Consequently, this author proposes that there will be a positive relationship between teacher professionalism and humanistic pupil control ideology.

Academic press, a third organizational climate index subtest, is described by Hoy and Sabo (1998) as the setting of high but achievable goals by teachers on the one hand and the positive response to those challenges by students on the other; with the principal exerting influence with the superiors and supplying needed resources. Humanistic pupil control ideology is positively related to classroom robustness (Estep, Willower, & Licata, 1980). Lunenburg (1983) found significant positive relationships between humanistic pupil control ideology and student motivation and with student overall self-concept as a learner ($R = -.51$, $p < .01$). It is therefore postulated that there will be a positive relationship between academic press and humanistic pupil control ideology.

Environmental press describes inside academic press (from the school) and outside environmental press (from the parents and the community) to improve schooling; indicating a strong pressure from parents and community to influence and change school policy and function. So long as this pressure does not diminish the importance of other professional considerations, it has been found to improve the academic achievement of children (Hoy, Hannum & Tschannen-Moran, 1998). Parental presence and involvement is expected to elicit humanistic considerations from teachers for their children. Teachers will tend to be humanistic if they perceive the parents as watching and involved. It is then logical to assume that there will be a positive relationship between environmental press and humanistic pupil control orientation in this study.

On the Relationship between Open and Healthy School, and Effectiveness

In their seminal work on climate, Halpin and Croft (1963) hinted on its importance in bringing about organizational effectiveness. Miles (1969) stated that an ineffective organization could never be healthy.

Hoy and Feldman (1987) also found that healthy schools have those characteristics of effectiveness like orderly environment, influential principal, trust and openness. Hoy and Sabo (1998) found zero order correlations between the dimensions of openness and health of school climate (OCI) and overall school effectiveness, with each making independent and collective contributions, explaining 48% of the variance (R = .70, p < .01). Invariably, in this study, it is expected that Organizational climate index, a comprehensive measure of openness and health will have a positive relationship to school effectiveness.

Collegial leadership another element of openness and health climate was defined as the principal's behavior that is open and supportive, but nondirective or restrictive (Hoy & Sabo, 1998). In their study involving forty-four elementary schools in New Jersey, Hoy, Tarter, and Wiskowskie (1992), found that supportive principal leadership has positive relationship to school effectiveness (r = .29, p < .05). Collegial leadership is a factor that describes principal's relationship with the teachers, which is both open and supportive, but nonrestrictive nor directive; it is principal's behavior that is both open and healthy. Consequently, it is predicted in this study that collegial leadership will be positively related to school effectiveness.

Teacher professionalism another dimension of openness and health depicts teacher collegiality in improving practice and getting better results (Sergiovanni, 1992). Collegial teachers trust each other, learn from one another, and are open to change. Hoy and colleagues (1992) found a strong positive relationship between "faculty trust in colleagues" and "effectiveness" and between "teacher collegial behavior" and "effectiveness" (r = .65, p < .01). Teacher professionalism encapsulates many of the teacher characteristics that are associated with school effectiveness such as teacher commitment to students, teacher trust in colleagues and student academic achievement (Hoy, Tarter, & Wiskowskie, 1992). It is therefore, expected that teacher professionalism will be positively related to school effectiveness.

Academic press is another openness and health climate subtest. Many authors have demonstrated connections between academic emphasis (which is identical to academic press) and student academic achievement (Bryk, Lee, & Holland, 1993; Murphy, Weil, Hallinger, & Mitman, 1982). Hoy, Tarter and Kottkamp, (1991) found a moderate correlation between academic emphasis and student academic achievement (r = .63, p < .01). Academic emphasis embodies those effectiveness characteristics cited by Edmonds (1979) as, orderly classroom environment, strong stress on academics and high student expectation. Hoy and Ferguson (1985) established a positive relationship between math, reading, and perceived school organizational effectiveness (r = .56; r = .50). It is therefore, highly anticipated that academic press will be positively related to school effectiveness.

Environmental press another element of openness and health, is a concept depicted by one variable, "institutional integrity", which indicates inside academic press and outside environmental press (Hoy & Sabo, 1998). Teachers do not like interference from parents or community, though it could sometimes work to the school's advantage by negatively contributing to students' academic achievement and school improvement (Hoy, Hannum, Tschannen-Moran, 1998). Hoy and Sabo (1998) found a zero order correlation between overall school effectiveness and perceived school effectiveness, and between environmental press and overall school effectiveness. Environmental press depicts outside parental and community press for school improvement, complemented by inside press from the principal and the teachers. It will be informative to see whether environmental press will be positively related to school effectiveness in this study.

On the Relationship between School with Humanistic Or Custodial Ideology, and Effectiveness

Although there are scarcities of literatures directly linking pupil control ideology to school effectiveness, there are no literature draught on studies that indirectly linked pupil control with school effectiveness. Hoy and Miskel (1996) contended that humanistic schools would have less alienated and goal-displaced students than schools with custodial orientation. Hoy (1972) equally found a relationship between custodialism and student's alienation. Custodial orientation was linked with closed school climate as humanistic orientation was related to open school climate; climate as openness is a characteristic of school effectiveness (Aplleberry & Hoy, 1969; Hoy & Sabo, 1998).

Hoy (2001) in a study of ninety-seven high schools in Ohio, found a negative relationship between enabling bureaucracy and custodial pupil control ideology of teachers, which inversely is a positive relationship with humanistic orientation of teachers (r = - .26, p < .01). Openness was positively related to perceived and overall school effectiveness (Hoy & Sabo, 1998). Cloer and Alexander (1992) found a significant difference between the principal's rating of effectiveness of humanistic inviting acts of teachers and custodial inviting acts [t (149.1) = 4.65, p. <. 01]. Humanistic inviting acts were more effective than custodial disinviting acts of teachers. Based on the above findings of implied or indirect relationship, this author is speculating that there will be a positive relationship between humanistic pupil control ideology and school effectiveness.

Climate as pupil control ideology (PCI) is not as complex as climate as openness and health (OCI) for the measurement of school environment. The organizational climate index (OCI), a combination of openness and health factors is based on solid framework and theory of Parsons, Bales, and Shils (1953), and has been tested over time and correlated with overall effectiveness (Hoy & Sabo, 1998). Given these empirical powers, it is expected that school climate as openness and health (OCI) will have an edge over school climate as pupil control ideology in their respective relationships to school effectiveness.

At the time of this study literatures were found on the relationship of openness and pupil control but none on organizational climate index and pupil control ideology. As the time of this study too, the author was also unaware of literatures directly linking climate as organizational climate index (openness and health) with pupil control ideology, or pupil control with school organizational effectiveness. It is believed that this investigation will contribute to theory, teaching and learning and would help in providing alternate routes to academic achievement and school effectiveness, as a by-pass to socioeconomic status, which cannot be so easily changed. The author sought to do this through a research study done in New York City public schools, an area with low socioeconomic status. Low socioeconomic status has been associated with low academic achievement, by demonstrating the importance of climate to school effectiveness this author will show its value as an alternative to socioeconomic status. In this study, the strength, richness and validity of climate variables will be measured with the criterion of effectiveness. It is therefore time to marshal out the hypotheses guiding this inquiry.

The Hypotheses

The relationships of organizational climates as openness and health, and pupil control ideology have been conceptually and theoretically delineated, their links and possible relationships with school effectiveness have been postulated; it is now necessary to set down the hypotheses guiding this investigation. In response to the above, these hypotheses are proposed:

Hypothesis 1: School climate as openness and health will be positively related to school climate as humanistic pupil control ideology.

Hypothesis 2: Collegial leadership will be positively related to humanistic pupil control ideology.

Hypothesis 3: Teacher professionalism will be positively related to humanistic pupil control ideology.

Hypothesis 4: Academic press will be positively related to humanistic pupil control ideology.

Hypothesis 5: Environmental press will be positively related to humanistic pupil control ideology.

Hypothesis 6: School climate as openness and health will be positively related to school effectiveness.

Hypothesis 7: Collegial leadership will be positively related to school effectiveness.

Hypothesis 8: Teacher professionalism will be positively related to school effectiveness.

Hypothesis 9: Academic emphasis will be positively related to school effectiveness.

Hypothesis 10: Environmental press will be positively related to school effectiveness.

Hypothesis 11: The school climate as humanistic pupil control ideology will be positively related to school effectiveness.

Hypothesis 12: The school climate as openness and health will make a greater contribution to school effectiveness than climate as humanistic pupil control ideology.

NOTES 1

The chapter on methodology and procedures involving data collections, sampling, instrumentation and descriptive statistics would have followed, but was moved to "Notes 2" at the end of the book after the conclusion in order not to overwhelm the reader with academic and statistical issues, but at the same time fulfilling the need for academic readers to view the research methods following the traditional routine of academic work. Readers who wish to follow the traditional order could go to the Notes 2 after the conclusion before reading the next chapter. The next chapter is on the results of tested hypotheses.

CHAPTER IV

Results of Tested Hypotheses, Discussions, Limitations, and Implications for Policy, Teaching and Learning

Results of Tested Hypotheses

PEARSON PRODUCT MOMENT CORRELATION analysis was used to test for the relationship between school climate as openness and health (OCI) and pupil control ideology (PCI), and also to test the relationship between OCI and effectiveness, and between PCI and effectiveness (see Notes 2, at the end of this book after the conclusion). A multiple simultaneous regression analysis was used to test for the greater predictor of effectiveness between OCI and PCI. The direction of pupil control ideology in this study was positive because items were scored positively.

The hypotheses were all supported by the empirical findings except for the relationships between *environmental press* and *pupil control ideology, environmental press* and *effectiveness*, and *pupil control ideology* and *effectiveness*. Hence, hypotheses 5, 10, and 11 were rejected, whereas hypotheses 1, 2, 3, 4, 6, 7, 8, 9 and 12 were confirmed (see Tables 7 & 8 for the results).

Unpredicted Significant Discoveries

In order to have a better picture of the actual relationship between the pupil control ideology (PCI) and the four measures of openness and health (OCI), the PCI was regressed on the OCI measures (academic press, collegial leadership, teacher professionalism, and environmental press). The result of the regression analysis revealed that only academic press was significant (see Table 9). Given the aforementioned result, academic press was then regressed on the other three OCI measures. With the exception of environmental press, all the other variables positively correlated with academic press (see Table 10 & Figure 4).

Discussion of Major Findings for Educational Policy, Teaching And Learning

On - the relationship between open and healthy school (OCI) and pupil control ideology (PCI)

Hypothesis 1 was supported; *openness and health (OCI)* was significantly related to *humanistic pupil control ideology*; an open and healthy school climate is also a school with humanistic pupil control ideology (See table 7). In other words, the more open and healthy the school climate, the more humanistic the teachers' pupil control ideology. The result is congruent with the findings of other scholars like Appleberry and Hoy, (1969) and Hoy and Henderson (1983), when they tested the relationship between the old openness instrument (OCDQ) and pupil control ideology (PCI). The findings of this study are based on the OCI measure, which is a combination of openness and health instruments, a more pervasive instrument than previous school climate measure. The finding of hypothesis one further re-establishes the positive relationship between openness and health and humanistic pupil control ideology (Hoy & Miskel, 1996). An open and healthy school climate goes along with a school in which the ideology of teachers' is humanistic.

School climate is described as a relatively enduring quality of the school environment, experienced by participants, which influences their behavior and is based on their collective perceptions of behaviors in the school (Hoy & Miskel, 1996). Open and healthy school climate is characterized by harmonious relationships among the technical level (teacher-student), the managerial level (principal), and the institutional level (school-parent-community) (Parsons, 1967). Pupil control is concerned with the social belief aspect of the school climate. It is the central motive or ideology from which students are viewed and a dominant guide to students' control. The relationship of openness and health with pupil control continues to point to the association between shared perception of behavior and shared ideology as described by Hoy and Miskel (1996). Pupil control is a form of school climate; it is the central aspect of school life and measures the school social climate in terms of the ideology dominating the control patterns among the faculty and between the faculty and the students. The promotion of an open and healthy school climate and humanistic ideology are both necessary for the school in achieving its goal, adapting to its environment and maintaining a cohesive workgroup and unique values, which are necessary factors for the growth, survival and development of any school (Hoy, Tarter & Kottkamp, 1991).

Hypothesis 2 was also supported; there was a positive relationship between *collegial leadership* and *humanistic pupil control ideology*. A little doubt was earlier entertained as to whether these two factors could be related based on the findings of previous researchers and the fact that pupil control is a teacher-student quality and not a principal-student factor (Estadt, Willower & Caldwell 1976). Although the predicted relationship was statistically significant, the relationship was low in degree. Consequently, pupil control was regressed on the elements of openness and health (OCI) and only academic press was significant (sees Table 9 & Figure 4). The correlation between collegial leadership and PCI was not significant, reaffirming the findings of previous researchers. Appleberry and Hoy (1969) did not find any significant difference between the humanistic ideology of principals in relatively open school climate and those in relatively closed school climate. Therefore, there was no other way of explaining the surprising significant relationship between *collegial leadership* and *pupil control ideology* in this study other than to attribute it to the intervening role of *academic press*.

The principal is not directly involved with pupil control in school. The relationship between collegial leadership and humanistic pupil control ideology is indirect. Academic press therefore, played a significant role in the aforementioned relationship. Hoy and Sabo (1998) described academic press as a factor that is loaded with principal-teacher, and teacher-student characteristics. As the person responsible for the academic progress of the school, the principal need to be a catalyst to humanistic teacher ideology. In order to perform the aforementioned role the principal has to be influential with the superiors and maintain instructional supplies; he or she needs to be open and supportive to the teachers, collectively and individually in meeting students' academic needs. Moved by humanistic considerations, thereof, teachers will then set challenging but achievable academic goals, and students will respond by working hard toward their academic progress. Therefore, the principal can only influence the school's effectiveness through collegial relationship with the teachers.

Hypothesis 3 was substantiated; *teacher professionalism* was positively related to *humanistic pupil control ideology*, which means that the greater the degree of teacher professionalism, the more humanistic the pupil control ideology. The result is congruent with previous findings. Willower and Landis (1970) associated professional orientation of teachers with humanistic ideology. Teacher professionalism is made up of *"teacher commitment"*, *"teacher collegiality"*, *"teacher affiliation"*, and *"teacher disengagement."* These are teachers' committed behavior to their students, their acquaintance with their teaching task, and their warmth, respect and friendliness with their colleagues. Hence, an on-going professional and instructional development, peer support, and collegiality and commitment to the teaching task are necessary to foster a professional climate and humanistic ideology amongst teachers (Glickman & Gordon, 2001). These will at the same time obviate custodial orientation in their relationship with their students.

Although the relationship between pupil control and teacher professionalism was significant in the zero order correlation, the regression analysis indicated that only academic press was significant (see Table 9 & Figure 4). Therefore, the relationship was most likely indirect and was mediated by academic press. Could it be that humanistic pupil control ideology must be oriented to academic achievement (academic press) so as to be related to teacher professionalism and vise versa? Without the press for academics, there would be no relationship between teacher professionalism and humanistic pupil control ideology.

Teacher characteristics are all significant components of academic press (Hoy & Sabo, 1998). Teachers challenge students by setting high but achievable academic goals; knowing that teachers really care, students respond positively to those challenges, by working hard and maintaining good results. Hence, humanistic acts of teachers must be properly directed so as to achieve the required learning objective. When students know one really cares, they will be ready to learn, but these caring humanistic acts must be oriented to academic press so as to be productive. It is therefore not a question of being nice to students but whether it has academic achievement objective. The relationship between teacher professionalism and pupil control ideology will be deliberated on later.

Hypothesis 4 was as expected; *academic press* was significantly related to *humanistic pupil control ideology* (see Table 9 & Figure 4). This result was anticipated because, microcosmically, academic press integrates teachers and pupils (teaching and learning), the major actors in pupil control ideology. Besides, academic press is an important quality of school productivity; the results of previous researchers pointed to similar direction. Humanistic pupil control ideology was related to student self-actualization, student motivation, and student overall concept as a learner (Diebert & Hoy, 1977; Lunenburg, 1983). Academic press was described by Hoy and Sabo (1998) as the setting of high but achievable academic goals by teachers on the one hand, and the positive response to those challenges by students on the other, with the principal exerting influence with the superiors and supplying needed resources. The function of the principal is indirect; he or she must be perceived as influential with the superiors in supplying the resources needed for instruction; which must be done in openness, friendliness and in supportiveness to the teachers. Teachers are then moved to commitment to both the teaching task and the students by setting high but achievable academic goals. Students' responses to those challenges are mediated by either the teachers' humanistic or custodial ideology. Teacher humanistic ideology encourages positive responses from the students and leads to classroom robustness as found by Estep, Willower, and Licata, (1980), high satisfaction with school as discovered by Schmidt (1992), and commitment to classwork as confirmed by Lunenburg and Schmidt (1989); teacher custodial ideology will produce opposite effects.

On - the relationship between open and healthy school (OCI) and effectiveness (IPOE)

Hypothesis 6 was as predicted; there is a positive relationship between school *openness and health,* and school *effectiveness*; in other words the more open and healthier the school climate, the greater the school effectiveness. The result was consistent with previous findings in which climate was positively related to effectiveness (Hoy & Sabo, 1998). Openness and health have been distinctively recognized as important elements of school effectiveness. Hoy and colleagues (1991) found that openness constituted a significant portion of effectiveness with a variance of 64% when compared with faculty trust. They also found that school health was a reliable predictor of school effectiveness, close to rivaling socioeconomic status. The OCI climate measure used in this research has the same strong theoretical base as the work of Parsons, Bales and Shils (1953), and the same link to academic achievement as the organizational health metaphor (Hoy, Tarter & Kottkamp, 1991). The result of this hypothesis was therefore, not surprising. The good news for school policy makers and administrators is that since it is easier to change school climate than to change students' socioeconomic status; the improvement of the instrumental and expressive needs of school climate would lead to greater school effectiveness. Hence, the enhancement of school climate remains the means and the end of school improvement and subsequently school effectiveness. Socioeconomic status has been a consistent predictor of academic achievement and school effectiveness, but could hardly be manipulated or changed; it is much harder to change the parental background of the students, parental education, income, and the children's upbringing, than to transform the school climate. Openness and health climate leads to school effectiveness when principal and teachers work together.

Hypothesis 7 was also validated; there was a positive relationship between *collegial leadership* and school *effectiveness.* Hoy and colleagues (1998) described collegial leadership as the principal behavior that is open and supportive, but neither directive nor restrictive. A little doubt was entertained earlier in this study as to whether both variables could be related. However, giving the low relationship of this result and the non-significant findings of previous researchers, a regression analysis was performed to get a clearer picture of the actual relationship of the two variables. The result indicated that collegial leadership was not significant with effectiveness, supporting the findings of Hoy and associates (1991, 1992), who surmised that open principal behavior would not necessarily lead to effective school unless it was coupled with open teacher behavior. Although the leadership role of the principal is important in an open and healthy school climate, its relationship to school effectiveness is indirect; teachers have more direct relationship to students and consequently, more direct role. Tarter, Hoy and Bliss (1989) had earlier remarked on the importance of the principal leadership as a catalyst for teacher commitment and school effectiveness. The principal is responsible for creating enabling climate in the school through the aid of the teachers. Principal's open, supportive and collegial behaviors would lead to greater trust and more professional behaviors among teachers, and subsequently greater academic progress and school effectiveness.

Hypothesis 8 was supported; there was a positive relationship between *teacher professionalism* and school *effectiveness*. Teacher professionalism depicts teacher collegiality in improving practice and getting better results (Sergiovanni, 1992). The findings of previous researchers have supported the notion that teacher professionalism encapsulates many of the teacher characteristics associated with school effectiveness such as teacher commitment to their students, teacher trust in their colleagues and student academic achievement (Hoy & Feldman, 1987; Hoy, Tarter, & Wiskowskie, 1992; Hoy & Sabo, 1998). Teachers are directly involved with the tasks of teaching and learning; they are the liaison between the principal and the students; they aid in transforming the input received by the school such as the students into a successful output, and so their role is irreplaceable. The result of this hypothesis indicated that the more professional the teachers, the more effective the school. The result of this hypothesis is congruent with previous findings between effectiveness, faculty-trust in colleagues, and teacher collegiality (Hoy et al., 1992). However, the result of the regression analysis indicated that only academic press was significant and it played a mediating role (see Table 10). Could it be that the only time teacher professionalism could fosters school effectiveness is when it is oriented to academic press? (see Figure 4). Academic press as earlier indicated embodies a lot of teacher characteristics. Teachers need to work together in setting high but achievable academic goals and in supporting the students toward the realization of those objectives.

Hence, teachers' friendliness, intimacy, trust, and enthusiasm among each other must lead to the goal of teaching and learning (academic press) in order to result to school effectiveness.

Hypothesis 9 was as expected; there was a positive relationship between *academic press* and school *effectiveness*; this result was highly anticipated. Therefore, the greater the degree of academic press, the more effective the school. Academic press depicts an orderly and serious learning environment; teachers set high but achievable academic goals and students work very hard to achieve them and respect those who get good grades; the principal exerts influence with the superiors and provides needed resources. Hoy and associates (1991) found academic emphasis to be correlated with academic achievement beyond the influence of socioeconomic status. Academic press has been noted as the greatest contributor to school effectiveness among climate dimensions beyond the impact of socioeconomic status (Hoy & Sabo, 1998). When the principal influences the superiors and plays his or her supportive role to the teachers; when the teachers are committed to teaching task and students by setting high but achievable academic goals; when the students respond to those challenges by working hard, an effective school is the outcome. Consequently, it could be said that the greater the degree of academic press, the more effective the school. Academic press was therefore, the single significant predictor of effectiveness among climate elements in this study. This finding reaffirmed the aim of education as teaching and learning, and academic press encapsulates that goal. As the focus of schooling, academic press involves the principal, the teachers, and the students; these are the major players in the productivity, adaptability, flexibility, and efficiency of the school as an organization. When these actors play together harmoniously in matching the school's expressive needs (human consideration) to its instrumental needs (academic orientation), the result is likely obvious: school effectiveness.

Hypothesis 10 was rejected; no relationship was found between *environmental press* and school *effectiveness*. Incidentally, this result did not agree with previous findings and could be attributed to a number of factors. Environmental press is a one positive variable depicting institutional integrity, indicating inside academic press and outside environmental press. There could not have been enough outside parental press and inside academic press to effect significant relationship in these New York City schools. It has been indicated that parents in poorer school districts are less likely to be involved in their children's schools. Parental and community press must be academically oriented and must be complemented with internal press from teachers and principal in order to improve schooling. Continuous research is needed on the nature of environmental press and its actual relationship to effectiveness.

On - the relationship between pupil control ideology (PCI) and effectiveness (IPOE)

Hypothesis 11 was uncorroborated; there was no correlation between *humanistic pupil control ideology* and school *effectiveness*. Some factors may have been responsible for this lack of relationship. Either the teachers in these schools were more custodial than humanistic or pupil control ideology (PCI) is not an element of school effectiveness or both. Pupil control is usually a problem in public schools especially in poorer school districts. Pupils did not choose to be there and teachers had no choice over the selection of their clients, all of which could foster custodial tendencies among teachers, leading to school ineffectiveness.

The result of the regression analysis indicated that only academic press was related to effectiveness and it also made a unique contribution to pupil control ideology. Therefore, the relationship of humanistic pupil control ideology to effectiveness is likely indirect and could be fostered by its relationship to academic press (see Figure 4). It has been said that pupil control is more a characteristic of teacher-student relationship (Hoy & Miskel, 1996). If humanistic teachers are committed to both their teaching task and their students by setting high but achievable academic goals, such positive responses like student high satisfaction with school, favorable teacher-student relationship, and student commitment to class work will lead to high academic achievement and greater school effectiveness (Schmidt, 1992; Lunenburg & Schmidt, 1989). Therefore humanistic pupil control ideology needs academic press in order to bear the fruit of school effectiveness.

On - the interrelationships among open and healthy school (OCI), pupil control ideology (PCI) and effectiveness (IPOE)

Hypothesis 12 was supported; the regression of *effectiveness* on *openness and health,* and *pupil control* indicated that climate as openness and health was a greater contributor to effectiveness than climate as humanistic pupil control ideology (R = .42, R Square = .18, Adjusted R = .13, p < .01). However, the results of the standardized coefficient beta indicated that academic press is a unique contributor among climate dimensions (see Table 8). Nevertheless, it was still corroborated that school climate as openness and health is a greater predictor of effectiveness than school climate as humanistic pupil control ideology, in spite of the fact that academic press played a unique role.

The general school climate involving openness, health and pupil control ideology had a great relationship to effectiveness with academic press as a unique contributor. Pupil control ideology is also a form of school climate (social climate) and so, the *general school climate* involving openness and health (OCI), and social climate (PCI) are predictors of effectiveness, and they can only do so in this poor school district with the mediation of academic press (see Table 8 & Figure 4).

Table 5

Descriptive Statistics of the Variables

Variables	Mean	Standard Deviation	N
Collegial Leadership	20.91	3.62	107
Teacher Professionalism	21.35	2.89	107
Academic Press	21.53	3.29	107
Environmental Press	12.02	1.77	107
Climate	75.81	8.03	107
Pupil Control Ideology	61.64	7.45	107
Effectiveness	3.35	.43	107

N = Number of schools

Table 6

Reliabilities of Organizational Climate Index, Pupil Control, and Effectiveness Dimensions

Variables	*Number of schools	Number of Items	Cronbach's Alpha
OCI	120	27	.91
CL	120	7	.93
TP	120	7	.92
AP	120	8	.87
EP	120	5	.65
PCI	117	20	.85
IPOE (EFF)	117	8	.90

*Only 107 schools were presented for analysis, the rest were list wise excluded
OCI = Organizational Climate Index (openness and health)
CL = Collegial Leadership
TP = Teacher Professionalism
AP = Academic Press
EP = Environmental Press
PCI = Pupil Control Ideology
IPOE (EFF) = Index of Perceived Organizational Effectiveness (Effectiveness)

Table 7

Pearson Correlation of the Independent and Dependent Variables
(N = 107)

Variables	CL	TP	AP	EP	OCI	PCI	EFF
CL	1.00	.50**	.49**	-.18	.79**	.22*	.24*
TP		1.00	.57**	-.15	.79**	.30**	.28**
AP			1.00	.00	.83**	.49**	.39**
EP				1.00	.09	-.08	-.12
OCI					1.00	.39**	.34**
PCI						1.00	.12
EFF							1.00

** = p < .01(significant at .01 alpha level)
* = p < .05 (significant at .05 alpha level)
CL. = Collegial leadership
TP. = Teacher Professionalism
AP. = Academic Press
EP. = Environmental Press
OCI. = Openness and health Composite (organizational climate index)
PCI. = Pupil Control Ideology
EFF. = Effectiveness

Table 8

Regression of Effectiveness on OCI and PCI Variables (N = 107)

Predictors	beta	Significant Level
Collegial Leadership	.02	ns
Teacher Professionalism	.06	ns
Academic Press	.39**	.01
Environmental Press	-.11	ns
Pupil Control Ideology	-.10	ns

Dependent Variable = Effectiveness

R = .42; R Square = .18; Adjusted R Square = .13; p < .01
* = p < .05 (significant at .05 alpha level)
** = p < .01 (significant at .01 alpha level)

Table 9

Regression of Pupil Control Ideology (PCI) on Openness and health (OCI) dimensions

Predictors	beta	Significant Level
Collegial Leadership	-.06	ns
Teacher Professionalism	.04	ns
Academic Press	.49**	.01
Environmental Press	-.09	ns

Dependent Variable = Pupil Control Ideology

R = .70; R Square = .49; Adjusted R Square = .47; p < .01
* = p < .05 (significant at .05 alpha level)
** = p < .01 (significant at .01 alpha level)

ns = non-significant

Table 10

Regression of Academic Press on Other OCI Dimensions

Predictors	beta	Significant Level
Collegial Leadership	.26**	.01
Teacher Professionalism	.36**	.01
Environmental Press	.13	ns

Dependent Variable = Academic Press

R = .70; R Square = .49; Adjusted R Square = .47; p < .01
* = p < .05 (significant at .05 alpha level)
** = p < .01(significant at .01 alpha level)
ns = non-significant

Figure 4

A Description of the relationship of Academic Press to other climate variables and its intermediary role to effectiveness

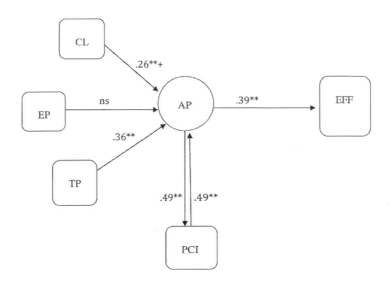

CL = Collegial Leadership
TP = Teacher Professionalism
PCI = Pupil Control Ideology
AP = Academic Press
EP = Environmental Press
EFF = Effectiveness
* = p < .05 (significant at .05 alpha level)
** = p < .01(significant at .01 alpha level)
ns = non-significant

Limitations of this Study

This is a correlational study and so the relationships established are not causal. The variables of Organizational climate Index (OCI), Pupil Control Ideology (PCI), and Index of Perceived Organizational Effectiveness (IPOE) are perceptual measures. They describe the state of affairs, which, however, reflect behaviors in schools. Students and principals were not included in the sample even though OCI also measures teachers' perception of students' and principal's behaviors. It might be necessary to find a way of including both principals and students in future research. No theoretical linkages explain the relationships in the PCI; it is a one-factor dimensional construct. However, it has proven to be a valid and reliable framework. The IPOE, though a subjective index of effectiveness, is valid and reliable, and is related to other measures of effectiveness (Hoy and Ferguson, 1985, Hoy and Sabo, 1998). It is a short-term measure in terms of time perspective. There may be a need to include intermediate and long-term time perspectives in future research.

Only hypotheses 5, 10, and 11 were uncorroborated, the rest were confirmed, although the results were low. The variables of climate as openness and health (OCI) and as pupil control ideology (PCI) together with effectiveness (IPOE) are useful tools for school improvement. In this study, the OCI and the PCI were not as robust as previous researchers have found, however, the regression analysis offered a clearer picture of the unique contributions of PCI and each OCI elements. Some factors could have contributed to the low data results. Data were collected from New York City public schools, mainly made up of inner city schools; this area had lower academic achievement than the suburban and rural school districts at the time of this research. Poorer school districts have been described as having lower levels of student achievement and poorer school environment than more affluent school neighborhood (DeBaryshe, Patterson, & Capaldi, 1993). Most of these schools were struggling at the time of this research. Moreover, public schools are service organizations in which clients are unselected and pupils' participation is mandatory, making it a little harder for teaching and learning. Pupil control is not just a dominant motif but an integrative concept giving meaning to teacher-teacher and teacher-student interactions (Hoy & Henderson, 1983). These factors may have contributed to the low correlation or lack of it as a few results have showed. Nevertheless, the fact that significant results were obtained in the relationship of OCI to effectiveness in spite of the apparent low socioeconomic status of the school district reaffirms the overall importance of openness and health climate both as a means and an end of school survival, development and growth.

Data for this study were part of archived data; such demographic information as gender, age, and years of experience were not available. These would have given more information on the nature of the samples. The school grade levels were mixed in this research; there were forty-eight elementary schools, thirty-six middle schools, and twenty-three secondary schools; the results would certainly differ on grade level bases if explored. Previous researchers have confirmed grade level differences in openness, health, and pupil control ideology (Kottkamp, Mulhern & Hoy, 1987; Lunenburg & Schmidt, 1989). Data were collected from urban school districts; the result would likely vary in suburban, rural, or richer school districts as confirmed by previous researchers (Lunenburg & Schmidt, 1989). However, the fact that it was conducted in a poor school district in New York, an area with low socioeconomic status, offers opportunity for inference in more affluent school areas. Furthermore, the fact that significant results were obtained in the relationship of school climate to effectiveness in spite of the apparent low socioeconomic status of the school district adds impetus to this study and reaffirms the overall importance of openness and health climate both as a means and an end, and as a functional alternative to socioeconomic status, in terms of improving teaching and learning and school effectiveness.

Implications for Educational Policy, Teaching and Learning

Academic Press as Encapsulating the Purpose and Major Actors of Schooling

According to the result, school climate as openness and health (OCI) is positively related to school effectiveness; meaning that the more open and healthy the school climate, the more effective the school. The OCI is founded on the reliable framework of adaptation, goal attainment, integration, and latency, which are the necessary effectiveness characteristics required by any school for survival, growth and development (Parsons, Bales, & Shils, 1953). The OCI also integrates academic press; academic press embodies those school effectiveness characteristics cited by Edmonds (1979) as orderly classroom environment, strong stress on academics, and high student expectation.

Academic press was a unique contributor to effectiveness among all the climate elements. This unique role was reflected by previous researchers, who demonstrated the powerful effect of academic emphasis (which is identical to academic press), and its unique relationship to effectiveness among climate dimensions, coming close to rivaling socioeconomic status (Hoy, Tatar, & Kottkamp, 1991; Hoy & Sabo, 1998).

When pupil control ideology was regressed on the other openness and health (OCI) elements, academic press made a unique contribution. When academic press was regressed on the remaining openness and health (OCI) dimensions, teacher professionalism and collegial leadership correlated significantly with academic press. Academic press was also the only unique contributor to effectiveness and had a singular relationship to almost all the openness and health dimensions and pupil control ideology. Hence, the relationships between the elements of climate as openness and health, and climate as humanistic pupil control ideology to effectiveness are determined by their relationships with academic press. It could also be said that the relationships between the dimensions of climate in general (OCI and PCI) and effectiveness are dependent on their relationships with academic press. Given the logic of interrelationships, academic press apparently plays a mediating role in the relationship between climate as OCI and climate as PCI, and in the general school climate's interrelationships with effectiveness (see Figure 4). Therefore, academic press is a necessary condition for the relationship of the general school climate (openness and health and pupil control ideology) to school effectiveness.

This study defined academic press as the setting of challenging but achievable academic goals by teachers, and students' positive response to those challenges, with the principal exerting influence with the superiors and supplying needed resources. Academic press encapsulates the major actors and activities required for academic achievement and school effectiveness. It involves the teachers, the students and the principal. The relationships amongst the principal, the teachers, and the students are the expressive needs (human relationship); whereas emphasis on academics is the instrumental need (academic press). Academic press integrates the facilitative role of the principal, the task commitment of the teachers, and the committed efforts of the students; it encapsulates the main purpose and the major actors of schooling as a process of teaching and learning.

The Interrelationships among Academic Press, Academic Achievement and School Effectiveness

The unique role of academic press in this study was reflected by previous researchers, who demonstrated the powerful effect of academic emphasis, and its unique relationship to academic achievement and school effectiveness among climate dimensions (Bryk, Lee, & Holland, 1993; Hoy & Sabo, 1998). Hoy and Ferguson (1985) established a positive relationship between math, reading and perceived school organizational effectiveness (r = .56 & r = .50). Many authors have demonstrated connections between academic emphasis and student academic achievement (Weil, Hallinger, & Mitman, 1982). Hoy, Tarter and Kottkamp, (1991) found a moderate correlation between academic emphasis and student academic achievement (r = .63, p < .01). What then is academic press? It was defined as the setting of challenging but achievable academic goals by teachers and the positive response to those challenges by the students, with the principal being influential with the superiors and supplying the resources that are needed, and the students respecting those who get good grades (Hoy & Sabo, 1998).

School climate has had influence over academic achievement for so many years, even when socioeconomic status was controlled as found in a longitudinal study by Hoy, Hannum, and Tschannen-Moran (1998). Smith, Hoy and Sweetland (2003) found a positive relationship between overall school climate and student academic achievement, with academic emphasis demonstrating a higher relationship. School climate is not only a good predictor of academic achievement but also of school effectiveness as shown in this very study. Just as academic press is a necessary condition for school effectiveness, likewise academic achievement, which is a criterion of school effectiveness. Therefore, no school can be effective unless its students are achieving academically; the former presupposes the latter, the latter is a precondition for the former. Consequently, students cannot achieve academically unless there is a consistent press for academics in the school, the latter also presupposes the former. Academic achievement is a precondition for school effectiveness just as academic press is a precondition for academic achievement. For every effective school there is high academic achievement, and for every academic achieving school there is high press for academics. This explains the reason why academic press is a necessary condition for effectiveness and for the relationship of other climate variables to school effectiveness in this very study.

Some people have been advocating alternative means for improving students' performance without academic achievement standard. The result of this study is saying that any criterion that deemphasizes academic press or academic emphasis is bound to fail, since it neglects the key element of schooling, and the main ingredient of teaching and learning.

Implications for Humanism and Discipline in School

Rosa is a fourth-grader; she attends a public school around the Northeastern part of the U.S. The school is made up of 69 percent African Americans, 16 percent Whites, and 15 percent Hispanics or Latinos. Students in this public school are mainly low income with 61 percent eligible for free or reduced-price lunch. The school has a student teacher ratio of 11:1. Rosa's teacher is very friendly and sociable and her students like her. She often allows the children to play in the classroom instead of bothering them with homework; she also makes sure her students are well fed during lunch. Rosa's teacher is known in the neighborhood, she is a regular in the neighborhoods social gatherings. She has been to Rosa's home a couple of times. However, her students are failing. Rosa performed bellow the national average in the National Assessment of Educational Progress (NAEP), and she is not alone. Student achievement in this school district is low; only 15 percent of students from the 4th grade to the 8th grade scored above average, in the National Assessment of Educational Progress in 2011. This is a typical example of humanistic teacher ideology that is not oriented to academic press. When a teacher plays nice with students with no academic press and academic objective in mind, the result is students' failure.

In this study, climate as humanistic pupil control ideology (PCI) has a positive relationship to academic press, and the PCI has an implied relationship to effectiveness through the mediation of academic press (AP). Hence, academic press appears to be a necessary and sufficient condition for humanistic pupil control ideology to lead to school effectiveness; and this has implication for niceness and discipline in schools. The integral role of academic press to teacher humanism addresses the issue of teachers who are merely playing nice with students without academic objective, leading one to conclude that it is not just about being nice and caring, but whether such congenialities are directed to academic achievement. Affection or humanism in school must be applied with academic aim and goal in mind. This may explain the reason why some nice and friendly teachers have poor performing students. If a teacher is nice and his or her students are not achieving academically, such a teacher has failed in terms of teaching and learning. Humanistic acts must contribute to the goal of teaching and learning for it to bear academic results. In her study on "What makes schools effective: A comparison of the relationships of communitarian climate and academic climate to mathematics achievement and attendance in middle school", Phillips (1997), found that academic climate measures are stronger than communitarian climate measures in their relationship to mathematics achievement and attendance. Therefore, if communitarian climate does not have the tone of academic press, it cannot lead to academic achievement or school effectiveness. Hence, humanistic acts of teachers must be properly directed so as to achieve the required learning objective. Humanistic acts should be right channeled to produce academic achievement results. Humanistic pupil control ideology must be geared toward academic press or be academic achievement oriented in order to lead to school effectiveness, otherwise, it is academically fruitless. Estep, Willower and Licata (1980) found humanistic pupil control ideology to be positively related to classroom robustness; Lunnenburg (1983) found it to be positively correlated to student motivation and overall self-concept as a learner.

DeBaryshe, Patterson and Capaldi (1993) found that students learn more and perform better in schools with a disciplinary climate necessary for teaching and learning. Taylor (2008) found that student achievement in reading is particularly related to student discipline and school safety. The findings of this study imply that such disciplinary acts must not only be viewed as humanistic or noncustodial, but must be oriented to the goal of teaching and learning; they should bear the print of academic press. School disciplinarians must ask themselves if their disciplinary acts are humanistic and possess the characteristics of academic press, or whether these acts can lead to classroom robustness and students' self-motivation, and overall self-concept (Estep, Willower

& Licata, 1980; Lunnenburg, 1983). Any school discipline that cannot improve learning or any school discipline that is not oriented to the goal of teaching and learning is ineffective and negates the goal of schooling. Willower, Eidell, and Hoy (1967) noted that custodial ideology is characterized by pessimism and watchful mistrust of students who are viewed as irresponsible and undisciplined people to be controlled with sanctions and punishments. Custodial schools are judgmental toward students' behaviors. In custodial schools, the stress on control and discipline is generally external; there is a pessimistic view of students as troublemakers (Willower, 1965). Humanistic pupil control ideology, in contrast, is characterized by trustfulness, and the understanding and acceptance of students as people who can freely learn; pupils who can make mistakes and improve on their behaviors. The model for humanism is a learning community in which behaviors are interpreted psychologically and socially rather than judgmentally (Nachtscheim & Hoy, 1976). Humanistic schools have optimistic view of students; emphases on discipline are placed on internal control of students rather than external. Disciplinary acts in humanistic schools are positive; they are the kind of tough love that is oriented to students' academic achievements, which have the elements of academic press and can lead to school effectiveness.

School Climate, an Easier and More Feasible Alternative to Academic Achievement than Socioeconomic Status

Eris was in second-grade at a public school in the North Midwestern part of the U.S. The school was composed of 70 percent Blacks, 5 percent Whites, 22 percent Latinos and 2 percent Asians; 1 percent considers themselves as belonging to other races. Students in this public school are mainly low income with 81 percent eligible for free or reduced-price lunch. The school was located in a poor but challenging neighborhood. By 2003, student achievement in this school district was low, with the school placed bellow the state average in math and reading; most students scored in the bottom quartile of the state assessment.

From 2004 to 2005, the school transitioned to a magnet school. Curriculum and textbooks were changed, new and competent principal and teachers were hired, teacher professional development was made more effective, there was integrative and effective parent involvement, and class sizes were reduced. There is now more extracurricular and after school intellectual stimulating programs. The school began to draw students from affluent neighborhoods in the surrounding area. The student population had become more integrated, with 42 percent Blacks, 31 percent Whites, 20 percent Latinos, 6 percent Asians and 1 percent of other racial groups.

The school had risen from an underperforming to a high performing school. The principal has administrative experience and is willing to work around the rules to attract and keep qualified teachers; she is an instructional leader and is more visible, involved and supportive of teachers' professional development. Teachers are experienced and have higher expectations of their students. They believe that every student can learn and go beyond their contract duties in taking responsibilities of their students' learning; they spend more time teaching mathematics, reading and science.

These teachers have pride in their school and are committed to their school progress; they have 97 percent attendance rate and feel responsible for their students' achievements and behaviors. Teachers work in collegiality with each other and with the principal; there is high morale and team spirit among the teaching force. The school has clear and effective disciplinary policy that is oriented to the goal of teaching and learning.

Students are now motivated to learn; there is healthy competition among the student population. Students know the expectation of their teachers and their parents; most of them are hoping to go to college. Teachers are in continual communication with their parents about the progress of their children in the classroom and areas they need improvement. There is a healthy parent school relationship. Parents are always welcome; they only have to check in at the office. Parents volunteer at the school and the principal and teachers are responsive to parents. The principal knows the neighborhood and is well known in the community. The school has parent outreach program and parent homework help line for parents who may be finding it difficult to help their children with their homework.

Even though her parents are poor and live in poor neighborhood, Eris made it to college and is hoping to be a teacher. Looking back she can see how her alma-mater had improved its climate to be more open and healthy; teacher ideology became more humanistic and students' academic performance improved.

Coleman and associates (1966) found that economic and social class was a major determinant of educational achievement and future success in a child's adult life. Since the debut of the aforementioned study, socioeconomic status became prominent, such that every educational processes and outcomes are increasingly predicated on socioeconomic criteria (Bornstein & Bradley, 2003). High socioeconomic status became the cure-all for academic achievement among some academic researchers and scholars (Sirin, 2005). This kind of perception destined the academic achievement of pupils and their future statuses in adult lives on the socioeconomic background of their parents.

Socioeconomic status was described as the hierarchical ranking of an individual or a family in terms of possession and influence over wealth, power and social status (Mueller & Parcel, 1981). Although there is no single agreed upon definition of socioeconomic status among researchers, many tend to agree, that it incorporates parental income, education and occupation (Gottfried, 1985; Houser, 1994).

The meta-analytical research of White (1982) on the relationship between socioeconomic status and academic achievement; and the follow up research by Sirin (2005) disproved some of the myths associated with socioeconomic status and academic achievement. Among the 200 studies reviewed, White (1982) found that when the individual student was the unit of analysis (the subject of measurement), there was a weak correlation between socioeconomic status and academic achievement (r = .22), but when the unit of analysis was aggregated (comprising of school and district factors), there was a strong correlation (r = .73). Other factors that mattered in this correlation (with the individual student as unit of analysis) were the *grade level, the type of socioeconomic and academic achievement measures used,* and *the year the data was collected.* Family characteristics (such as, *home environment*) often referred to as socioeconomic status had also a significant correlation with academic achievement when the individual student was the unit of analysis (r = .55). White's findings (with the individual student as the unit of analysis) showed a weak correlation with traditional indicators of socioeconomic status (which are, *parent income, occupational level, and educational attainment*), but strong relationship with grade level and home environment.

In order to replicate Whites study Sirin (2005) tested for the relationship between socioeconomic status and academic achievement, and the effects of students and methodology in the previous research. Data were collected from studies published from 1990 to 2000, which included 101,157 individual students, 6,871 schools, and 128 school districts. The result showed average to strong correlation between socioeconomic status and academic achievement. This relationship was however, dependent on the following: the unit of analysis, the characteristics of socioeconomic status and achievement measures used, the school level, the minority status of the student, and the location of the school. Unlike White's study, which showed the effect of grade level diminishing as the student progresses, Sirin found that the relationship between socioeconomic status and academic achievement increased until middle school and stabilized in high school. Sirin equally discovered that for minority students, family background (such as parental income, occupation, and education) was less predictive of academic achievement than the neighborhood socioeconomic status factors. Sirin also found that the relationship between socioeconomic status and academic achievement was stronger for non-urban schools, but weaker for urban schools; this was consistent with other research findings (Wilson, 1996). One major problem with socioeconomic status is that it cannot be easily changed, necessitating the need to look for a more workable route bypassing socioeconomic status.

In their correlation and multiple regression analytical study (involving school climate, socioeconomic status and students achievement), Hoy and Sabo (1998) found the following results: For Mathematics achievement, socioeconomic status had a *Beta* of .44 (p < .01), *Environmental press* had .30 (p < .01), and *Academic press* had .27 (p < .01). For Reading achievement, socioeconomic status had a Beta of .44 (p < .01), *Environmental press* had .30 [p < .01], *Academic press* had .22 (p < .01) and Collegial *leadership* had .19 (p < .05). Therefore, one can reasonably say that although socioeconomic status is a better predictor of academic achievement in the aforementioned study, climate variables were equally good, and did not lag behind. Individually the climate dimensions had significant but independent effects on academic achievement; cumulatively they rival socioeconomic status. Therefore, school climate is a good predictor of academic achievement, and presents a functional alternative to socioeconomic status which cannot be easily changed.

The findings of this study showed that the general school climate (openness and health and pupil control ideology) has a relationship to school effectiveness and by implication student's academic achievement. Hoy and Sweetland (2003) found that there is a positive relationship between overall school climate and student academic achievement. Among the climate elements, academic emphasis correlated with academic achievement beyond the influence of socioeconomic status (Hoy, Tarter and Kottkamp, 1991). School climate has therefore proven to be both the means and end of school effectiveness and students' academic achievement. Climate has those strong characteristics required by any school to survive, grow, and develop, and these are adaptation, goal attainment, integration, and latency (Parsons, Bales, & Shils, 1953). School climate has also those qualities that help a school accommodate to its environments, set and implement its goals, preserve cohesive systems, and create and maintain unique values among its members (Hoy, Hannum, & Tschannen-Moran, 1998).

Socioeconomic status has been a good predictor of academic achievement and school effectiveness, but could not be easily manipulated or changed; it is much harder to change the parental background of the students, parental education, income, and children's upbringing, than to transform the school climate. Since it is easier to change the school climate, than to alter student's socioeconomic status, the improvement of the former appears to be a less difficult route to school effectiveness and by implication, student's academic achievement. It is much easier to change schooling, teaching and learning than to change parent's income, educational attainment and neighborhood. Therefore, the academic achievement of children is not destined on their parent's socioeconomic status. Children from low socioeconomic status background are not destined to fail either in academics and or future status in adult life. The reason why parents send their children to school is for them to be taught and for their children to learn; schools have greater roles in these responsibilities. School districts who found themselves disadvantaged by socioeconomic status can find solution in raising their school climate. On the other hand, school districts that have the advantage of high socioeconomic status can excel by continuously making their schools more open and healthier. The enhancement of school climate remains the means and the end of school improvement and subsequently school effectiveness. An open and healthy school climate integrates high academic press, high student academic achievement and school effectiveness (Hannum & Tschannen-Moran, 1998). School climate incorporates academic emphasis by which teachers set challenging but achievable academic goals and students responds positively to those challenges, with the principal exerting influence with the superiors and supplying needed resources. O'Day and Bitter (2003) made a review of schools identified for improvement in Washington state, in which schools which made improvement were compared with those that did not. The authors found that development of coherent and coordinated instructional program was a major factor for schools which improved and exceeded their academic goals. Those schools placed emphasis on academics, which led to their improvement. School climate encapsulates academic emphasis (academic press) which integrates the major actors and activities required for academic achievement and school effectiveness. The relationships amongst the principal, the teachers, and the students (human relationship) are the expressive needs, whereas academic emphasis (academic press) is the instrumental need. School climate incorporates teacher humanistic acts and perception of students as people who can freely learn and take responsibilities for their actions. In a humanistic school climate, students are cared for and motivated to learn, school discipline is put in the proper perspective.

CHAPTER V

Other Implications and Suggestions for Educational Policy, Teaching and Learning

The Effect of Teacher Efficacy on Students' Academic Achievement

Academic press encapsulates the major actors and activities required for academic achievement and school effectiveness. It also integrates the facilitative role of the principal and the task orientation of the teachers. Teachers are directly involved with the tasks of teaching and learning. Teachers are the liaison between the principal and the students; they aid in the transformation of the school's human input into a successful output, and so, their role is irreplaceable. Students' long exposures to poorly qualified and low efficacious teachers in their formative years ultimately lead to lingering poor academic achievements. Students lose interest and morale when exposed consecutively to low efficacious and poor performing teachers. Students from low income and minority communities are mostly affected by the aforementioned phenomenon, since they were already carrying the burden of low socioeconomic statuses (Land- Billings, 1994; Ferguson, 1998). As a construct, 'teacher efficacy' evolved from the concept of the locus of control of Rotter (1966) and the social cognitive theory of Bandura (1977). However, an integrative model for measuring teacher efficacy was developed by Tschannen-Moran, Woolfolk Hoy, and Wayne K. Hoy (1998). Hoy and Miskel defined teacher efficacy as, "teacher's belief in his or her capacity to organize and execute courses of action required to successfully accomplish a specific teaching task in a particular context" (2005, p. 153). The concept of teacher efficacy varies from one context to another and from one situation to another. For a teacher to be efficacious in judgment, "consideration of the teaching task and its context are required as well as an assessment of one's strengths and weaknesses in relation to the requirements of the task at hand" (Hoy & Miskel, p. 154). Teacher perceptions of self-efficacy feed itself in a cyclic phenomenon of progress or retrogress. In judging his or her efficacy, a teacher should usually balance his or her competence and capabilities in terms of strength and weakness within a particular teaching environment. Higher teacher efficacy improves performance, which in turn increases efficacy; lower teacher efficacy decreases performance and ultimately results in decreased teacher efficacy. A teacher's strong sense of self-efficacy has a positive relationship to students' learning and students' achievements (Ashton, 1985; Amor, Conry-Oseguera, Cox, King, McDonnell, Pascal, Pauly, & Zellman, 1976).

Hoy and Woolfolk (1993) made a distinction between teacher personal efficacy and teacher general efficacy. These authors contended that both the personal attributes of teachers and their perceptions about the school help in creating their sense of personal efficacy. In this same aforementioned study, they found that there is a relationship between school climate and teacher efficacy; with academic emphasis and principal influence being the most significant of the climate measures after controlling for other variables. Goddard (2001) found that collective teacher efficacy increases student academic achievement. Consequently, for the promotion of teaching efficacy, teachers need to "(a) set high but achievable goals, (b) create an orderly and serious environment, and (c) respect academic excellence" (Hoy & Woolfolk, 1993, p. 365). In order to help teachers accomplish these goals, the principal needs to exert influence with the superiors, be responsive and supportive of teachers, and provide needed classroom supplies. These aforementioned characteristics are attributes of academic press and academic achievement. It is by these actions that the principal can improve both the personal and collective efficacy of teachers. The principal merely enables teacher's self-efficacy through his or her influence and supportive behaviors. The development of teacher's strong sense of self-efficacy has a long term pay off in the academic development and achievement of the students.

Teacher educational level has also been found to be significant in building teacher self-efficacy (Hoy & Woolfolk, 1993). Hoover-Dempsey, and Bassler and Brissie (1987) while using a different construct, found teacher efficacy to be significant with the perceptions of parent's support (r = .60 < .01). The authors defined teacher efficacy as, "teachers' belief that they are effective in teaching, that the children they teach can learn, and that there is a body of professional knowledge available to them when they need assistance" (1987, p. 421). Efficacious teachers, who are sure of themselves, believe in their ability to involve parents without a feeling of inadequacy or a feeling of being threatened. Inefficacious teachers who are unsure of themselves feel intimidated or inadequate to reach out to parents and involve them in the academic progress of their children. Teacher's sense of self-efficacy and principal's influence and belief in teacher efficacy are among the factors that affect the school's organizational climate; these in turn affect students' academic performance. Just as teacher self-efficacy is related to academic achievement of the student (Ross, 1992), collective teacher efficacy is also found to be related to students' academic achievement in math and reading (Goddard, Hoy & Hoy, 2000; Tschannen-Moran & Barr, 2004). Collective teacher efficacy is the teachers' shared perception as a group regarding their group performance (Bandura, 1997). To be effective, a school must be open and healthy, with the principal offering needed support to teachers and teachers believing in themselves and their students, with teachers working together in collegiality, and parents helping to bridge the learning gap between the school and the home. It is only within these aforementioned academic and home environments that students can consistently learn and achieve. High efficacious teachers have high expectations of their students, these teachers are ready to teach individual student in a way he or she can learn and achieve academically.

The Burden of Poverty, Minority Status, Poor Neighborhood, and Students' Academic Achievement

Natasha is an 11 year old African American student in fifth grade at a public school located in a poor neighborhood in the Southwestern part of the U.S. The school's ethnic compositions are 70 percent Latinos, 20 percent Blacks, 8 percent Whites and 2 percent Asians. She has a sister sibling who is of a different father. Her mother a recovering drug addict has been clean for the past 1 year and works at a fast food restaurant and a local bar to support her children. Her father has no job and has just been released from the state penitentiary having served two years for cocaine related issues. Natasha's school has a high student teacher ratio and large class sizes; there is less individual attention for each student. The school library has older and fewer books; the school building and the school play ground are poorly maintained. The classrooms have poorly maintained infrastructures; the school environment is less motivating for learning. The school is failing, standardized test scores are subpar; teachers are less qualified, less experienced and less paid; there is low student expectation among the teachers. Teachers have low morale and often complain that most of their students are disruptive in the classroom that some others have language problems and that their parents are uncooperative. The principal rarely visits the classrooms; he is always busy in his office, sometimes visiting the school board for one problem or the other. There are fewer extracurricular activities, few school nurses and social workers. Natasha has many friends in her school, her former teacher said that 'she liked going to school but lacked motivation at home'. Her present teacher who is merely buying time and hoping for a transfer is not interested in her academic progress; consequently, Natasha's interest in schooling is waning and she seemed to have forgotten most of the things she learned from her previous teacher. Natasha and her family live in a challenging neighborhood where they have to deal with drugs, street gangs and gun violence. The grocery stores in this neighborhood have a lot of junk food; there are rarely a store nearby where one can buy fruits and vegetables. Natasha's mom gets home tired from her two jobs, and has little interest in helping her daughter with her school work; having been a high school dropout, she finds anything academic very intimidating. The story of

Natasha is an example of the challenges being faced by many poor, racial minority children who live in poor neighborhoods.

Poverty, economic disadvantaged racial minority status and poor neighborhood are burdens for higher academic achievement. Sirin (2005) suggested a number of factors as being responsible for the lower academic achievement of minority students in the United States; these are that "Minorities are more likely to live in low-income households or in single parent families; their parents are likely to have less education; and they often attend under-funded schools" (2005, p. 420). Some of the aforementioned are aspects and extensions of socioeconomic status (SES), which have been associated with educational achievement (Ma & Klinger, 2000). Bankston III and Caldas (1998), in their study on "Family structure, schoolmates, and racial inequalities in school achievement" found negative relationships between minority status, poverty, parental education and single headed family structure, and academic achievement. They also found that schools with larger concentration of minority students are likely to do poorly academically. Most of the parents in these neighborhoods have poor paying jobs, and have to do many odd jobs that pay little in order to survive; they also have the added burden of living in challenging neighborhoods where there are scarcities of academic stimulating programs. Under these condition, there may be hardly enough time and disposition for these parents to devote to the academic work of their kids. This author wishes to offer solutions on what needs to be done to obviate the burden of minority status, poverty and the attendant poor neighborhood on students' academic achievement.

Students who come from poor parental background are more likely to go to schools with limited resources. Most children who live in poor neighborhoods have little or no social services that stimulate academic performance; they have to grapple with street violence, diseases, drug trafficking, street gangs and other social maladies. A good number of these inner city kids come to school far behind their mates in affluent districts, incapable of identifying basic numbers, colors, and alphabetical letters; some of these children are not used to sitting in structured settings and are more often than not bearing the burdens of special academic needs. Parents who have a choice of neighborhood could move out to safer environments with low educational risk factors. Parent who cannot would have to brace up to counter the high educational risk factors associated with poor and minority neighborhoods by limiting its negative influence on their children, and creating an educational enabling home and family environment. Such parents would have to start early by making their homes environment academic friendly, providing home cognitive stimulating resources, limiting the time their children watch television and hang out with peers on the street, engaging their kids in after-school programs, tutoring and summer school sessions, taking them to local libraries and to intellectual stimulating field trips. Low socioeconomic status parents who have the choice can also take their children to well-funded and better-equipped schools. Data from the National Assessment of Educational Progress consistently showed that children in affluent suburban schools have greater academic achievements than those in urban (disadvantaged) schools (Sirin, 2005). However, parents must be involved in their children's education and know how their children are doing in school; they need to network with their class teachers and follow up with their children's activities in school. Teachers have to involve parents in the academic activities of their children and elicit their help in bridging the gap between school climate and the home climate.

Researchers have however noted that it is much more difficult for low socioeconomic status parents to be involved in the education of their children than higher socioeconomic status parents, this may also be due to a sense of intimidation and past negative experiences they themselves may have had with school (McNeal Jr. & Ralph, 2001; Lareau, 1987). For some of such parents, the school is an unfamiliar terrain. Moreover, most of these parents do the menial jobs that take more time and pay less, with some having to do more than two of such jobs to be able to feed their family and pay their rents thereby being absent from their children most of the time. The help of teachers are needed in these aforementioned circumstances. It requires committed and high self-efficacious teachers to engage the involvement such parents in the academic activities of their children. This requires passionate and committed teachers who can go the extra mile for the interest of their students. Such teachers are motivated by the need to help their students learn, and grow into successful adults. The reason why parents send their children to school is for them to learn and become successful in life. Since it is the responsibility of teachers to know the best way to bring this out in each child, teachers should be able to help in the diagnosis of the academic problem of each child, and find the best way to elicit the continuous support of their parents, so as to bridge the gap between the school and the home. Kober (2001) in a report to the Center on Education Policy of Washington, DC, found that although Racial-ethnic differences in family income is a factor in the achievement gap between students, it did not totally explain it. She found that schools factors contributed to the gap, which among others include the fact that minority students were not fully participating in rigorous courses, that their instructions were watered down, that their teachers were less qualified and experienced, that their teachers have low expectations of their students, that resources were not equitable for high minority schools compared to others and that their school climate was less conducive for learning. Kannapel and Clements, with Taylor, and Hibpshman (2005) in their comparison of eight high-performing and high-poverty schools in Kentucky which had closed their achievement gap with those that had not, found that these schools scored high in safe and orderly environment; they also scored high in these areas: expectation of students, teachers acceptance of their responsibilities in student successes and failures, assignment of teachers according to their abilities, regular communication with families, caring for students, pricing and celebration of students achievements, commitment to fairness, and appreciation of diversity. Therefore the school has a major role to play in obviating the academic burden associated with low socioeconomic factors and teachers have primary responsibility in this regard. Hauser-Cram, Warfied, Stadler, and Sirin (2005) in their study on "School environment and the diverging pathways of students living in poverty", found that minority students in high-poverty elementary schools with positive climate progress to middle schools with greater achievement.

The Effect of Teacher Expectation on Students' Academic Achievement

School climate as already indicated integrates 'academic press', which embodies those effectiveness characteristics cited by Edmonds (1979) as, orderly classroom environment, strong stress on academics, and high student expectation. Student expectation is a factor of climate and of school effectiveness. The Pygmalion study of Rosenthal and Jacobs (1968) sets the stage for the study of the impact of teacher expectation on learning. The expectations of teachers matter a lot in the academic performance of their students. Low teacher expectation leads to low academic achievement, high teacher expectation leads to high academic performance. When teachers are committed to both their teaching task by setting high but achievable academic goals raising their expectations of their students, the dividends are students' higher academic achievements. Teacher humanistic ideology encourages positive responses from students, leading to classroom robustness, high satisfaction with school, greater commitment to class work, and greater academic achievement and school effectiveness (Estep, Willower, & Licata, 1980; Schmidt, 1992; Lunenburg & Schmidt, 1989; Hoy & Sabo, 1998).

One of the attributes of academic press that makes it so effective for academic achievement is that of 'teacher expectation'. According to Lee and Smith, "The level of expectations held by a school's teachers for students is a 'brick' upon which the structure of academic press for (or relaxation of) academic goals is built" (1999, p. 913). The powerful and the sole predictive effect of academic press in this study collaborates the findings of these aforementioned researchers on the impact of teacher expectation on students academic achievement. The effect of teacher expectation is more noticeable with minority students, and much more with younger children (Goodlad, 1984; Ladson-Billings, 1994). Teacher expectation was found to have more impact on younger children than on older children because it is at this level that children are developing self-concept and self-image (Raudenbush, 1984). Children are more impressionable and vulnerable when they are younger than when they are older. Teacher differential expectations and treatments of some students in terms of race, ethnicity, religion, sex, socioeconomic status, language pattern and personal habit, affect their academic achievements. Low expectations seem to have more drastic effect on lowering students' academic performance than high expectations do in raising their performance. Although only five to ten percent of student's performance is attributable to teacher differential expectation, its accumulative effects on a student over a long period of time, can do a lot of good if the expectation is high and positive, and a lot of damage if it is low and negative (Brophy, 1983). When teachers set high but achievable academic goals for their students and communicate those goals in positive ways, treating each student in an equal and humanistic way, students' academic achievement increases. The results of studies on teacher expectation could be of practical importance in raising teachers' awareness on how to communicate positive and unbiased expectations to students (Kerman & Martin, 1980; Guskey, 1982). A good teacher is also one who can understand, how each student learns, their strengths and weaknesses.

The Importance of Learning Styles for Students' Academic Achievement

Although, there are general or universal characteristics of learning common to all, there is unique or specific individual learning styles. People have a few learning commonalities, but individuals have unique learning styles. Dunn and Dunn defined learning style as, "the way in which each learner begins to concentrate on, process, and retain new and difficult information" (1992, p. 2). Learning style is the natural ways each student obtains information, processes it, maintains it, retains and uses it. The learning style technique of Dunn and Dunn is based on two distinct learning theories: the Cognitive theory and the Brain Lateralization theory. Keefe defined learning style as the, "cognitive, affective, and physiological traits that serve as relatively stable indicators of how learners perceive, interact with, and respond to the learning environment" (1982, p. 44). Learning style is a set of factors, which includes behaviors, and attitudes facilitating learning for every individual within a given situation. Every student has a very unique style of learning and every teacher has a distinctive learning style. Teachers teach the way they learn and students learn according to their learning styles, which they are most comfortable with, "One teacher may use abstract examples while others may use concrete illustrations...Teachers should understand their own learning style but must use a variety of ways to accommodate the learning styles of their students" (Thompson, Orr, Thompson, & Park, 2002, p. 2). By becoming familiar with the students' learning styles teachers and parents can more easily recognize the strengths and weaknesses of their wards, harness the strengths and compensate for their weaknesses.

Students learn differently at different rates and styles. No particular learning style is superior to the other, hence, as far as intelligence is concerned, learning style is neutral. However, traditional school structure seems to favor certain styles above others, which could be one of the reasons why some students are lagging behind academically. Students' performances in different subject areas are also based on how each student learns, and students' academic achievements are related to their unique learning styles. When teachers teach with approaches and resources that are in conformity to every student's learning style, there is increased academic achievement (Miller, Always & McKinley, 1987; Dunn, Dunn, Primavera, Sinatra, & Virostko, 1987). Consequently, the structure of the school and teachers' instructional techniques should be configured to afford students with varying learning styles equal chances of success.

Dunn and Dunn's decades of research on learning styles revealed that learners are affected by certain elements such as: environmental factors (learning with sound, light, a certain room temperature and room design), emotional factors (learning by motivation, learning with persistence, learning with a sense of responsibility, learning within structured or self-styled environment), sociological factors (being by oneself, learning in pair, learning with peers, with a team, an adult or varied), physiological factors (learning by perception, with intake, learning at a certain time of the day, or learning by mobility), and psychological factors (being a global or analytic learner, being a hemispheric, impulsive or reflective learner) (1992, p. 5). The learning style is based on these premises: that every individual has a style of learning, which is measurable, that people learn more and better with their learning styles, that each individual has his or her strengths and people have different strengths, that everyone can learn, that the learning environment, resources and techniques respond to different learning styles, that teachers can use leaning style resources in their instruction, and that students can harness their learning style abilities and strengths (Dunn & Dunn, 1992, p. 6).

Students who were classified as poor achievers or dropouts, students who were said to have disciplinary problems and students from poor neighborhoods and lower socioeconomic statuses have shown reversal in academic achievement when instructions were designed to their learning styles (Andrew, 1990; Matthews, 1991). Hence, "when students are taught through their identified learning style preferences, they evidence statistically increased academic achievement, improved attitudes toward instruction, and better discipline than when they are taught through their nonpreferred styles" (Dunn & Dunn, 1992, p. 3). This is a source of encouragement for parents and teachers who had mistakenly believed that their children or students cannot learn as a result of accumulated burdens of poor neighborhood and low socioeconomic factors.

One fact about learning styles techniques is that it requires supportive principals, committed teachers and dedicated parents. There is no doubt that in order to teach to every student's learning styles there is need to double efforts in the school and at home.

Teaching to every student's learning styles can lead to a process of customized, personalized and teacher-pupil interactive learning, which requires creative and committed teachers. Great schools and teachers are those who are willing to go the extra mile in raising the standards and rising up to the challenge.

The Effects of Self-concept, Self-efficacy, Self-esteem, on Students' Academic Achievement

It is merely overstating the obvious stressing the importance of self-concept, self-efficacy and self-esteem to academic achievement. Each of them has a relationship to the other, and all are related to the academic achievement of students (Gordon, 1997). Students' self-concept and self-efficacy are important mediators and precondition for learning and academic achievement (Pajares, 1996; Skaalvik & Akaalvik, 2004).

Our beliefs are our generalizations and assumptions about our world, which we individually hold to be true and these motivate our behaviors. These beliefs help us attribute causes to events, give explanations to our behaviors and make judgments about our abilities and efforts. Among these beliefs are those of self-perception, which are self-concept, self-esteem and self-efficacy among others. Your self-concept is, "the sum total of your attitudes and beliefs about yourself, the kind of person you are, your likes and dislikes, and what you are or are not capable of doing well" (Maddux, 1999, p. 231). Self-concept is a bunch of beliefs people hold about themselves. A person's self-esteem is the person's estimation of his or her worth and how much the person likes the kind of person he or she thinks himself or herself to be. Self-concept, self-esteem and self-efficacy are different concepts although each one affects the other. Two people may have similar self-concepts but divergent self-esteems. Your belief about your self-concept will affect your self-esteem only if such a belief is important to you. In the same way if your self-efficacy is highly valuable to you, it will contributes to your self-esteem. If getting a high grade is important to a child and valuable to him or her and the child has a self-concept of being very good at it, it will contribute to the child's self-esteem. The child's belief in his or her ability to make good grade no matter the odds is his or her self-efficacy. If beating deadline in accomplishing a task is important and valuable to a student, and the student has a self-concept of being good at it, it will help to the student's self-esteem; the student's belief in himself or herself regarding such ability is his or her self-efficacy.

Self-efficacy is a very powerful behavioral motivational belief system in any person's life from day to day (Hoy & Miskel, 2005). Self-efficacy theory states that, "psychological and behavioral changes can be explained best by examining our beliefs and expectations about our ability to achieve important goals, deal effectively with obstacles that stand in the way of those goals, and master or overcome the problems that come our way of life" (Maddux, 1999, p. 231). This theory received conceptual twist from Bandura (1977; 1986; 1991). Self-efficacy is, "a person's judgment of his or her capability to organize and execute a course of action that is required to attain a certain level of performance" (Hoy & Miskel, p. 150). Self-efficacy is one's assessment of his or her ability to perform a task. Through self-efficacy, students are motivated to set their personal goals, decide how much effort they will expend and make determination as to whether they will withstand difficulties and failures and or be resilient enough to achieve those goals.

Children build their self-efficacy over time through feedback received from performances, previous historical experiences and influences from parents, teachers, peers and the society. *Mastery experience* is the most crucial source of self-efficacy; it results from actual experiences of successes and failures (Hoy & Miskel, 2005). Continuous failures lead to self-doubt and reduce self-efficacy, whereas constant successes raise self-belief and self-efficacy. For example, a student who has consistently failed to make his grades will be dealing with self-doubt in the classroom and during examination; consistent failures lower his or her self-efficacy. On the other hand, a student who has consistently made excellent grades in the classroom believes in himself or herself; consistent high grades boost his or her self-efficacy. *Modeling and vicarious experience* are facets of self-efficacy that affect self-perception through knowledge and social comparison. Through knowledge one learns how to do things by watching an expert or someone who knows better. A person can raise his or her self-efficacy through social comparison with successful people of similar social group (Hoy & Miskel). Children learn from one another and challenge one another; a poor performing kid could receive a self-efficacy boost if placed among peers who work harder. A child will receive a self-efficacy increase if placed in the classroom of a teacher who believes in himself or herself. *Verbal persuasion,* another source of self-efficacy is a process of being motivated verbally by an external agent into believing that you have what it takes to achieve, if you try harder, and develop your skills and knowledge (Wood & Bandura, 1989; Hoy & Miskel). An example is a parent, talking their child into believing that he or she has what it takes to make better grades in school and excel in life. Such a parent usually begin early to get involved in their child's education by cooperating with the school, having discussion with their kid about school work, helping and overseeing the child's homework, providing academic stimulating program at home, moderating television viewing and peer activities, using tough love to communicate the value of learning, self-discipline and the spirit of hard-work, and positively passing on their academic and life's expectations on the child while making sure these are in harmony with their child's expectations and goals. Through verbal persuasion, teachers with high expectation could motivate their students into doing better in school work. Parents and teachers should use verbal persuasion to communicate their expectations to their wards.

Emotional arousal, another source of self-efficacy is the condition that positive psychological factors such as, anticipation, enthusiasms and exhilaration can boosts ones self-efficacy in contrast to negative factors such as, dread, panic, weariness, tension and nervousness. Continuous failures may be associated with a certain negative feeling of nervousness. For example, the arousal of unpleasant emotions whenever a student is making a speech or reading in the classroom reduces his or her self-efficacy. Even when the student had advanced in speaking or reading in class, such unpleasant feeling may still arise because of its association with negative past behaviors. In order to remedy such a situation, there is need to recognize and address such past experiences before there could be an improvement on student's self efficacy. Invariably, continuous successes may be associated with positive feelings of conquest, which can lead to the arousal of a feeling of enthusiasm when a student remembers past successes.

High self-efficacy is the hub of a student's drive, determination, perseverance, and resilience, whereas, low self-efficacy is the center of his or her self doubt, incompetence and loss of faith himself or herself. By building your child's self-efficacy, you are also elevating his or her self-concept and self-esteem. Every parent and teacher needs to help in making the student believe in himself or herself. Some children have been beaten down because of past consistent failures; these children need a lot of emotional support, academic assistance and motivational encouragement in order to start believing in themselves again. These motivational boosters have to come from both school and home, the teacher and the parent; the home and the school climate need to work together to encourage a child towards academic success.

Self-esteem, an aspect of self-concept, is, "a person's broadest evaluation of him or herself" (Baumeister, 1999, p. 341). Low self-esteem is a person's lack of firm positive belief about himself or herself. People with high self-esteem have a high self perception. On the average, people with high self-esteem are not necessarily different from people with low self-esteem; it's mainly a matter of perception. People with high self-esteem perceive themselves as better, more beautiful or handsome, and smarter in comparison with people with low self-esteem, which boosts their performances. Uplifting a student's perception of his/her self-confidence can improve the child's self-esteem. "Self-confidence is a belief in abilities, while self-esteem is the value placed on those same abilities" (Mboya, 1988, p. 197). Raising a student's self-esteem will require making him or her change his or her belief and perception about himself or herself. A student's self esteem is increased when the student stays around people and environment that affirms and challenges him or her; taking the student away from people and environment that put them down can also help the student reclaim his or her self-esteem.

Having a bad teacher over a period of time can kill the academic interest of a child. Parental low expectation can also wane the academic passion of a child. A student's self-confidence is boosted when the student has a motivating teacher and supportive parent.

All these self-perception categories (self-concept, self-esteem and self-efficacy) can be general and specific. There is general self-concept, and particular self-concept. Students may have a low self-concept in academics but a high level of social or physical self-concept. Some students who do very well in sports or athletic activities but poorly in academics may have a high physical self-concept but low academic self-concept. It has been established that academic self-concept has more significant relationship to academic performance than the general self-concept (Byrne, 1990). For a student to achieve academically, the self-concept support and encouragement system must be zeroed to the areas of academic performance and achievement.

The Need to Bridge the School Climate and the Home Climate, for Students' Academic Achievement

The U.S. Department in *The Longitudinal Evaluation of School Change and Performance (LESCP) in Title I Schools* (2001a) found that the poverty of individual student and school had negative effects on student achievement; it also found that students performed poorly in mathematics in schools with higher percentage of poor students. Poorer school districts were described as having lower levels of student achievement and poorer school environment than more affluent school neighborhoods (DeBaryshe, Patterson & Capaldi, 1993). Most of these New York City public schools seem to be struggling at the time of this study; nevertheless, the fact that significant results were obtained in the relationship of climate to effectiveness in spite of the apparent low socioeconomic status of the school district, and student background reaffirms the overall importance of climate as a means to students' academic achievement. Failure is therefore not a destiny for children from low socioeconomic status background. In their study on high-performing, high-poverty elementary schools in Kentucky, Kannapel and Clements, with Taylor, and Hibpshman (2005) found that these school climate factors were related to academic success: high student expectation, principal-teacher collaboration in decision making, staff and faculty care, parent-teacher communication, high faculty morale and high faculty work ethic, strong instructional and academic focus, and staff strategy coordination.

It has already been noted how the meta-analytical findings of White (1982) and Sirin (2005) had challenged the myth that socioeconomic status (SES) is a cure-all for academic achievement as some researchers have made us to believe. White (1982) found a weak correlation between the traditional measures of socioeconomic status and academic achievement, but a strong correlation with grade level and home environment.

In the aforementioned studies of both White (1982) and Sirin (2005), certain factors of the home played mediating role in the relationship between socioeconomic status and academic achievement. White found that the home environment (among other socioeconomic status factors) had strong relationship with academic achievement, and "is considerably more powerful than parents' income and education in influencing what children learn in the first six years of life and during the twelve years of primary and secondary education" (Walberg & Paik, 2000, p. 7). Consequently, the home environment could be isolated, as a more pliable alternative to student academic achievement, than parental income and education, among other socioeconomic factors. Therefore, tinkering with the home environment, a major factor of socioeconomic status could be an additional way of breaking the jinx of failures associated with low socioeconomic status for low academic achieving pupils. Among the socioeconomic status' elements, the home environment appears to be the most pliable and flexible, therefore, improving the home environment and making it more open, more academic friendly and supportive could be a better way of helping underachieving kids than changing the other socioeconomic status factors.

School climate offers conceptual clarity for the description of the atmosphere or the feel of the school (Halpin & Croft, 1963). School climate was described as those characteristics that distinguish one school from another, which influence the behaviors of its members, and give the school its personality (Forehand & Gilmer, 1964; Tagiuri, 1968). School climate is marked by openness, healthiness and humanism. An open, healthy and humanistic school climate is known for its academic emphasis. School climate is therefore a distinctive quality of school environment (Cheng, 1991; Stewart, 1979). Hoy and Miskel constitutively defined school climate as, "a relatively enduring quality of the school environment that is experienced by participants, affects their behavior, and is based on their collective perceptions of behavior in schools" (1996, p. 141). Borrowing from the above concept, the author of this study will define home or family climate as those enduring distinctive characteristics of the home environment that distinguish one home from another, which influence the behaviors of its members, which is based on their collective perception of behaviors and give the home its personality. An open and functional home climate should be known for its positive communication of parental academic expectations to children and open discussion of those expectations with children; it should also be known for stimulating academic programs, moderation of television viewing and external peer activities; it is marked by parental cooperation with teachers, modeling of learning values in children, and instilling self-discipline and the spirit of hard work in children. Such a home climate should be distinguished by sound human relationship and task orientation or by sound social capital and academic capital.

This author is therefore inclined to postulate that both the factors of the school (school climate) and the factors of the home (home climate) are needed for integral students' academic success. It has already been shown how the school climate elements of openness and health, and humanistic pupil control ideology are related to the academic achievement of the school. It is expected that an academically open home climate have positive educational characteristics needed by a child's to start schooling. There is need then, to bridge the gap between the home and the school, between the home climate and the school climate. Either of these factors is a necessary but not a sufficient condition for a holistic academic climate needed by a child for academic progress. The school must liaise with the home and the home must support the school. These factors must work together to maximize students' academic potentials and minimize their academic liabilities. The academic enhancement of the school and the home climates will increase both the intellectual and social capital needed to boost a child's academic achievement. What was learned at school would be forgotten if the home did not reinforce it, and what was taught at home would be derailed if the school did not strengthen it, so there is need for continuity. A healthy home and school climates are together, sufficient conditions for a sustainable student's academic performance. These factors must work together to maximize overall students' academic success and minimize their academic liabilities. Both factors must liaise to minimize the low academic risk factors associated with low socioeconomic factors and maximize the high academic advantages of high socioeconomic factors. One of the ways the home can support the school in raising the academic achievement of the child is through parental involvement.

The Importance of Early Parental Involvement on Student Academic Achievement

Most low academic achieving children start school with high academic risk baggage; in order words, they were already behind in academic capital, because of the effects of low academic resources in their upbringing environment (Evans, 2004). If we want children to achieve in school, families need to be academically oriented and focused in their children's development. There should be early academic intervention in the child's upbringing from the home to the daycare and the preschool. Parents should not view their child's education as different from their child's upbringing. Children are taught to speak, eat and walk; they are also taught when to brush their teeth and when to go to bed; these are all part of education. Children's academic upbringing should not be viewed as different, or separate; it is part of the process of learning in the child's upbringing. Parent's who view their child's schooling as different from the process of their upbringing make a great mistake. Making the child's environment academic friendly and teaching the child the right way is part of their academic journey.

Children spend their waking hours away from school and a greater piece of their life with their parents (Clark, 1990). Hence, parents have great influence on their children, for according to Walberg and Paik, "One major reason that parental influence is so strong is that, from infancy until the age of 18, children spend approximately 92% of their time outside school under the influence of their parents" (2000, p. 7). Researchers have consistently shown that the earlier involvement of parents in their child's education the greater the effects on the child's subsequent academic achievement (Fan, 2001; Fan & Chen, 2001). There is also a general belief by 86% of the public that parental support is one of the most effective ways of improving the school (Rose, Gallup, & Elam, 1997), hence, "Educators at all levels know that successful students—at all ability levels—have families who stay informed and involved in their children's education" (Epstein, 2007, p. 16). Walberg (1984) in his review of studies on parent-school programs found that family participation in a child's education is twice as predictive of students' academic achievement as the socioeconomic status of the family. Besides, "Dozens of studies have shown that the home environment has a powerful effect on what children and youth learn within and outside school. This environment [home environment] is considerably more powerful than parents' income and education in influencing what children learn in the first six years of life and during the twelve years of primary and secondary education" (Walberg & Paik, 2000, p. 7). Fan and Chen (2001), through a meta-analytic method, discovered that the major constructs of parent's involvement are parent expectations and parenting style, parent supervision and communication. Parent expectations and parenting style appeared to be the most crucial and the most consistent predictors of students' academic achievement in the aforesaid research. The authors further noted that parent expectations must be positively in agreement with students' perception of those expectations in order to lead to students' academic success. Hao and Bonstead-Bruns (1998) postulated that there must be agreement between the educational expectations of the parent and that of the child in order to bring about the child's educational achievement. Therefore, shared parent and child educational expectation increases the child's learning and educational achievement. The encouraging news of this finding is that disadvantaged children and children of low socioeconomic status can learn if their parents can be involved early in their educational development and infuse academic elements in their home environment. Children can achieve academically if their parents can provide academic stimulating programs at their homes, encourage their children academically, cooperate with their children's teachers, have discussions with their kids about their school work, help and oversee their children's home work, moderate their wards television viewing and peer activities, use tuff-love to model the value of learning in their children, instill self-discipline and the spirit of hard-work in their children, and positively communicate their academic expectations to their kids, which of course must also be in agreement with their children's self-academic expectations. Children will learn when they know you care and support their academic endeavors. Most kids who drop out of school have already dropped out from their homes even before they reached school, because of lack of adequate academic support at their homes. The continuous lack of parental involvement retrogressively widens the gap between the school and the home. Through parent meeting, the school can help parents in areas where their children are failing and where they need improvement. Through training the school can help parents on the skills they need to partner with the school in the education of their children. Parents can be involved as chaperon or volunteers in their children's classrooms. Parents can be invited to their child's classrooms to talk about their careers and jobs. Parents can donate age appropriate books to their children's classrooms and can be encouraged to borrow books from the school to read for their children.

Hoover-Dempsey and Brissie (1987) found that school's socioeconomic status (SES) was significant in predicting aspects of parents' involvement (parent conferences, volunteering, and teacher perception of parents' support) but insignificant in home-based parent involvement indicators (parent involvement in tutoring at home and carrying out teacher designed home instruction programs). Hence, although it is true that higher socioeconomic status parents are more inclined to be involved in their children's schooling and partner with their kids' teachers; lower socioeconomic status parents who have interest and determination can equally do so. Such parents need a feeling of confidence, motivated by their desire for their children's success. Professional teachers and teachers with high self-efficacy who are committed to the academic success of their students are known to positively liaise with their students' parents without feeling inadequate or threatened. The academic relationship between the home and the school must be improved to enhance students' academic performances (Hobbs, Dokecki, Hoover-Dempsey, Moroney, Shayne, & Weeks, 1984). The family and the school have shared responsibility for the academic success of the students, "families and schools must engage in frequent, confident, and complementary transactions if each institution is to contribute all it can to the socialization and education of children"

(Hoover-Dempsey & Brissie, 1987, p. 431). Committed teachers and parents should be mindful of the need to create a triad relationship (teacher-student-parent) for the academic improvement of the pupils. The African saying still holds: "it takes a village to raise a child".

The Role of Communities and Governments in Students' Academic Achievement

Openness and health of school climate integrates academic press or academic emphasis, which embodies those effectiveness characteristics cited by Edmonds (1979) as orderly classroom environment, strong stress on academics, and high student expectation. Academic press depicts an orderly and serious learning environment in which teachers set high but achievable goals and students work very hard and respect those who get good grades, with the principal exerting influence with the superiors in supplying needed resources. Many authors have demonstrated connections between academic emphasis and student academic achievement (Bryk, Lee, & Holland, 1993). Hoy, Tarter and Kottkamp, (1991) found a correlation between academic emphasis and student academic achievement ($r = .63$, $p < .01$). Governments, both national and local, and the community have great responsibilities in the education and educational achievement of its young citizens. Education of pupils is the responsibility of the parents, teachers, communities and the governments. The provision of sound education is a basic human right for every child; therefore, any government that does not take the education of it pupils seriously is grossly irresponsible. A huge sum of the government budget should be devoted to the education of its young citizens.

There can be no orderly and serious learning environment if the structural resources are not there; neither can the principal supply needed resources if they are not provided by the government and the community. Even when all these resources are put in place, there is need for the right thinking and acting personnel to manage and implement them. It is the role of government to construct new schools and renovate old ones, provide instructional resources and support, hire qualified principals and teachers and ensures they are well paid, provide safe environments, network and involve private corporations, structure the curriculum and create effective standards of measuring academic achievements and school effectiveness. Teachers need to be well paid, they also need job security in order to give their best to the education of their students, but tenures should not jeopardize teaching and learning. Unreasonable tenures should not be maintained to the detriment of children academic achievement and growth. The government should create effective standards of measuring teacher performance and negotiate with teachers to find a better way of reconciling tenure with academic achievement and school effectiveness so that the purpose of schooling is not defeated and the academic growth of pupils not compromised; priority should be given to the academic performance of students.

A major way of helping inner city schools or schools in poor neighborhoods improve is for the state and the local government to come to their aid providing adequate financial resources to keep enough qualified teachers, increasing public safety in the schools' environments, reducing class sizes, raising the standard of infrastructures in the schools, and demanding but also rewarding accountabilities and higher performances from the principals and teachers. It is the role and responsibility of government to move educational resources where it is most needed within the state, city or community. In a circumstance where the burden of home climate leads to insurmountable academic risk, a situation could be arranged where kids would have longer school days. The local or state governments would have to provide financial assistance in building and sponsoring a public school with longer school hours, after-school programs, weekend exciting intellectual stimulating activities and summer school programs; the government has to provide cognitive stimulating programs such as tutoring, visitation of local libraries, and social activities, games and sports. Students would be dropped off at their neighborhoods in the evening for their parents to pick them up and be brought back the next day. Schools of this sort could arrange for enticing weekend cognitive and creative activities to keep kids intellectually going. The financial support of the government and the community, the committed efforts of the principals and teachers, and the dedicated work of the parents are needed for such a program to be successful. The aforementioned program can work when these bodies want to invest on the education of its pupils, giving it priority.

Early intervention is better than remedial measures to save a poor achieving kid; it is easier to intervene when children are younger and more malleable than when they are older; the former would require less efforts and fewer resources. However, it can never be too late to save underachieving schools or pupils. The effects of the environment on human intelligence are felt early in a child's development (Bloom, 1964). Any intervention whose purpose is to boost the academic achievement of a pupil must be introduced early in the child's upbringing (McLoyd & Duke, 1998). Children carry the burden of socioeconomic status to adult life only when such disadvantages are allowed to linger by parents, schools, communities and governments. The school has a greater role to play in this regard because the reason why students are sent to school is for them to learn and grow into successful adults.

CONCLUSION

The school and the family as open systems were the conceptual underpinning and overarching framework of this study. An open system involves interacting elements that acquire inputs, transforms them, and generates outputs to the environment. An open system entails human and material rudiments, quantitative and qualitative elements in an on-going interaction.

School's openness and health climate and pupil control ideology integrate the transformation of input in the school's internal process and structures. School effectiveness is a performance outcome measure; not only is it diffused within the input and transformation of resources; it is an end product of such interactions.

Climate as openness and health and as pupil control are qualities of "system harmony" of the school, the key to the acquisition of external resources and the means for their transformation. A school with harmonious cooperation and collaboration in its internal systems cannot but be highly effective. The mode, manner, and quality of the input (the means) of a school's climate affect the performance-outcome (the end) of its operation.

The results of this study established the relationships between climate as openness and health (OCI) and climate as pupil control ideology (PCI). Pupil control is an aspect of school climate that measures the teachers' motif towards students' control, a social climate of the school. Since it is easier to change school openness and health climate than to change teachers' pupil control ideology (social climate), school leaders and teachers could pursue this process as an easier way of realizing an effective school. Nevertheless, by improving the openness and health climate of a school its humanistic pupil control ideology is also enhanced.

The result of this study also demonstrated that there was a

relationship between school climate as openness and health (OCI) and effectiveness (IPOE), and between the general school climate (OCI and PCI) and school effectiveness. The relationship between openness and health and effectiveness was not as robust as those found by previous studies. It could be that public schools in New York City as at the time of data collection were solving the basic and imperative functions of adaptation, goal attainment, integration, and latency but with a low degree of effectiveness, and were not properly meeting their instrumental and expressive needs (Parsons, Bales & Shils, 1953). All school board, leadership and instructors should be mindful of the need for a more harmonious relationship between the managerial (principal), the technical (teachers and pupils) and the institutional levels (parents and community) in addressing students' academic needs for a greater degree of school effectiveness.

Nevertheless, the fact that significant results were obtained in the relationship of climate as openness and health, the general school climate in their interrelationships to effectiveness (in spite of the apparent low socioeconomic status of the school district and student population) reaffirms the overall importance of climate both as a means and an end. School districts, principals and teachers who found themselves disadvantaged by low socioeconomic status of their neighborhood can find consolation in raising their general school climate. An open general school climate integrates high academic press, humanistic teacher control ideology, high student academic achievement and school effectiveness.

Among all the climate elements, academic press was intermediary in the relationships amongst pupil control ideology, openness and health, and effectiveness. It was apparently the most significant and consistent predictor in the relationship among openness and health (OCI), pupil control ideology (PCI), and school effectiveness. Therefore, the improvement of a school's academic press, or a strong emphasis on academics could be an easier way of fostering the school's openness and health, its pupil control ideology, and subsequently, its effectiveness. Emphasis on academics is necessary for students' academic achievements and school effectiveness. The press for academics is conditional for humanistic acts of teachers to bear academic results, it is also necessary for disciplinary acts to be academically effective. The school is a place of teaching and learning, emphasis on academics typifies that goal. All school's activities must bear the stamp and the seal of academic press, whose goal is academic achievement and school effectiveness.

Socioeconomic status has been a good predictor of academic achievement and school effectiveness, but could not be easily manipulated or changed; it is much harder to change the parental background of the students, parental education, income, and the children's upbringing, than to transform the school climate. Since it is easier to change school climate, than to alter student's socioeconomic status, the improvement of the former appears to be a less difficult route to school effectiveness and by implication, student's academic achievement. It is much easier to change schooling, teaching and learning than to change parent's income, educational attainment and neighborhood. Therefore, the academic achievement of children should not be destined on their parent's socioeconomic status. Children from low socioeconomic status background are not destined to fail either in academics and or future status in adult life. The reason why parents send their children to school is for them to be taught and for them to learn; the school has greater role in these responsibilities.

However, an open home climate is a healthy environment for the academic development and growth of a child. Children spend most of their waking hours at home and carry both the burden and the advantage of home environment to the school. Parents need to be involved early in the academic development of their children. Parents have to create an enabling home environment, a healthy academic climate, and a functional family environment that responds to the academic needs and growth of the child.

Open system harmony, viewed as shared perception and shared ideology is necessary for a more effective school and a functional home. The school and the home as open systems must work together towards the acquisition and fostering of the academic and social capitals needed by a child for academic achievement. The academic relationship between the home and the school must be improved to guarantee sustainable student academic performance. The factors of the home (home climate) and the factors of the school (school climate) are integral for a holistic student academic success. The gap between the home and the school or between the home climate and the school climate should be bridged for students' academic achievements. The school needs to liaise with the home and the home has to support the school; teachers have greater role in initiating and bringing this about. These factors must work together to maximize the students' academic potentials and minimize their academic liabilities. The family and the school have shared responsibilities for the academic success of the student, consequently, both must engage in regular, positive, and collaborative transactions if either institution is to give all it can to the socialization and education of the child.

Parsons, Bales, and Shils (1953) postulated that social systems must solve four basic problems in order to survive, grow, and develop, and these are, adaptation, goal attainment, integration, and latency; meaning that social systems must accommodate to their environments, set and implement their goals, preserve cohesive systems, and create and maintain unique values among its members (Hoy, Hannum, & Tschannen-Moran, 1998; Hoy, Tartar & Kottkamp, 1991). The solving of these basic functions is imperative for all social systems including the school and the family. Therefore, in order to survive, grow, and be effective, the school and the family must adapt to their environments, achieve their objectives, and infuse common values and solidarity into their members (Hoy & Sabo, 1998). "Adaptation and goal achievement" are categorized as *instrumental needs,* whereas "integration and latency" are described as *expressive needs* (Hoy & Feldman; Parsons, 1967). A social system that cannot adapt or achieve its goals looses its reason for existence, whereas the one that cannot integrate its members loses them. For a healthy academic performance of the child and his or her future success in life, the school and the family have to create enabling environment marked by trust, warmth and interest in the child; an environment that attends to his or her social needs, a climate that is task and academic orientated. Such an environment should be respectful of the child, and be aimed toward the academic growth of the child and his or her success in adult life.

NOTES *2*
METHODOLOGY AND PROCEDURES

Population Used for this Study and Data Sampling

Samples for this research were part of archived data collected from New York City public schools: elementary, middle, and secondary. The <u>Directory of Public Schools and Administrators in New York State</u> was used to obtain the initial list of all public schools in New York City. The New York City Board of Education School-Based Personnel division was then contacted, and with their database, a list of schools with forty or more teachers was generated. By an initial screening some schools were dropped because of the wide variation of instructional programs. These were schools with less than forty teachers, charter schools, collaborative schools, alternative schools, vocational schools, and schools administered by the New York City Board of Higher Education.

Elementary and middle schools were sorted by districts; high schools were sorted by number followed by a letter designating borough; for example, X for Bronx borough, M for Manhattan, K for Brooklyn, Q for Queens, and R for Staten Island borough. Sixty schools were randomly selected through a protocol. The number of schools obtained was divided by sixty, and a frequency count was made. Through the frequency count, every third school was selected, and these were the schools chosen for the study. To adjust for skew, modifications were made following an analysis of representative Title I schools and School-Wide Project schools for each borough (Title I schools receive funds from the federal and state grants. School-Wide Project schools have autonomous budgets with a little supervision from the district and have powers of discretion on the use of school funds).

After the selection of sixty schools from each of the grade levels for the study, senior staff members of St. John's University contacted the Deputy Chancellor of the New York City Board of Education seeking permission to do the study. This request was granted and the cooperation of the chief executive staff was guaranteed. This protocol was necessary to ensure the representativeness of the local district superintendents, the building principals, and the staff in the survey.

Procedures Used for Data Collection

The survey instruments used in this study were part of a larger project called "The Chancellor's Cohort Study." The School of Education and Human Services of St. John's University New York carried this out. The Chancellor's Cohort was a group of New York City supervisors, selected in 1997 by the Board of Education to pursue doctoral studies in Educational Administration at St. John's University.

A sub-group of this Cohort packaged the questionnaires and apportioned 180 sets of protocols comprising 60 elementary schools, 60 middle schools, and 60 high schools, for delivery and eventual pick up. Cohort members or their designees who were properly instructed distributed questionnaires on a staff development day. The purpose of the research was explained. Anonymity and confidentiality were guaranteed and ensured, and participants signed an authorization in this regard. Those who did not wish to participate had the option to decline. There were a minimum of five sets of protocols. In order to save time and to check for response bias, one quarter of the faculty responded to each questionnaire. The responses were subsequently collected. About 10, 000 teachers were surveyed. After the initial collection of data, further data collection was necessary to resubmit incomplete surveys and also to increase the number of participating schools. The later collection was done in December 2000, with an explanatory letter to the schools. Surveys were administered to schools in the usual manner as in the previous data collection. These were collected at regularly scheduled faculty meetings and were very successful.

This pool of data among others contained data for the school climate as openness and health (OCI) and climate as pupil control ideology (PCI), and effectiveness used in this research. Usable samples contained 120 schools for OCI, 117 schools for PCI, and also 117 schools for effectiveness (IPOE). From this pool of data, 107 schools were listwise retained to test the hypotheses of this study. These were schools presenting data in all the variables. They comprised 48 elementary schools, 36 middle schools, and 23 secondary schools; there was no discrimination for grade level in the analyses.

Instruments and Measurements Used for this Study

Data were collected with the *Organizational Climate Index* (OCI), the *Pupil Control Ideology* form (PCI), and the *Index of Perceived Effectiveness* (IPOE). The OCI and PCI were used to measure the independent variables, and the IPOE was used to measure the dependent variable.

Data for climate as openness and health were collected with the Organizational Climate Index (OCI), a short form index of openness and health, developed by Hoy and Sabo (1998). It is a 30-item Likert-type instrument with four point scales ranging from "rarely occurs" to "very frequently occurs." Examples of the items are, "The principal explores all sides of topics and admits that other opinions exists." "Parents press for school improvement." "Teachers are committed to their students." "Students try hard to improve on previous work." (Hoy & Sabo, 1998). The instrument was validly and reliably tested by a correlation and regression analyses with student achievement (in Math, Reading, and Writing), socioeconomic status (SES), and overall effectiveness. The OCI samples for this study have a Cronbach's alpha of .91 for 120 schools. The OCI dimensions and their Cronbach's alpha were as follows: *"collegial leadership"* .93, *"teacher professionalism"* .92, *"academic press"* .87, and "environmental press" .65 (see Table 6).

Data for pupil control ideology (PCI) were collected with Pupil Control Ideology form, a 20-item Likert-type instrument. This instrument was originally developed by Gilbert and Levinson (1957), but adapted by Willower, Eidell and Hoy (1967) for the measurement of the pupil control orientation of public school staff. The typology has polarities ranging from "custodialism" to "humanism", designed to tap the custodial and the humanistic ideological frameworks of schools. It had split half reliabilities range from .91 - .95. Willower and colleagues

91

also supported its validity by comparing the results with those obtained from the principal's judgments of teachers' ideology. The PCI is a one directional 20-item Likert-type instrument, with scales ranging from "strongly agree" to "strongly disagree." Items were scored and summed in the custodial direction (negative direction). Examples of such items are, "A few pupils are just young hoodlums and should be treated accordingly." "Being friendly with pupils often leads them to become too familiar." "Pupils often misbehave in order to make the teacher look bad." (Willower et al., 1967). The instrument was meant to generate a range of scores from 20 to 100, the higher the score the more custodial the respondent's orientation (less humanism). Negative significant custodialism inversely means positive significant humanism.

The PCI samples for this research have a Cronbach's alpha of .85 for 117 schools (see Table 6). Items were reversed and scored in the humanistic direction (positive direction). The instrument generated a range of scores from 20 to 100, and the higher the score, the more humanistic the respondent's orientation (less custodialism). The direction of pupil control ideology in this study was made positive rather than negative. Items and scores were aggregated on school level, and the dimension of the *pupil control Ideology* (PCI) was computed for analyses.

The Index of Perceived Organizational Effectiveness (IPOE) is an 8-item index originally developed by Mott (1972) but modified by Miskel and colleagues for use in schools (Miskel, McDonald, & Bloom, 1983; Miskel, Fevurly, & Stewart, 1979). The school's overall effectiveness was measured along the dimensions of quantity and quality of the product, efficiency, adaptability, and flexibility. Subjects responded to a five-point scale, with questions on how much, how good, how well, how flexible, or how quickly their school achieved the eight identified objectives. The alpha coefficient of reliability was .89 and it had extensive indications of validity (Miskel et al., 1979). Examples of the items are, "Of the various things produced by the people you know in your school, how much are they producing?" "When changes are made in the methods, routines, or equipment, how quickly do the people in your school accept and adjust to the changes?" "How good a job do people in your school do in coping with emergencies and disruptions?" The Cronbach's alpha for the IPOE samples of this study was .90 for 117 schools (see Table 6). Scores were calculated and items were aggregated on school level. The effectiveness dimension (IPOE) was then computed for analyses.

Descriptive Statistics

Since the variables involved in this study were organizational properties, the school was the unit of analysis (Sirotnik, 1980). The organizational climate index (OCI), pupil control ideology (PCI), and perceived organizational effectiveness (IPOE) items were aggregated by school level; scores were calculated to reflect school organizational properties. The aggregates were the *openness and health composite (OCI)*, the four factors of Organizational climate index (*collegial leadership, teacher professionalism, academic press, and environmental press*), the *pupil control ideology* (PCI), and *effectiveness* (IPOE).

A descriptive statistics was computed for all the samples (see Table 5). A hundred and seven (107) schools were listwise presented for analysis; in other words, only the schools that presented data in all the variables were retained for statistical investigation. The predictor (independent) variables were the openness and health composite (OCI) and dimensions, and the pupil control ideology (PCI). Effectiveness (IPOE) was the dependent variable (see Table 5).

Checking for Reliabilities

After running the reliabilities, climate as openness and health (OCI) had a Cronbach's coefficient alpha of .91 for 120 schools. The alpha coefficients of reliabilities for the various dimensions of OCI were .93 for "collegial leadership," .92 for "teacher professionalism," .87 for "academic press," and .65 for "environmental press." Climate as pupil control ideology (PCI) had a Cronbach's alpha of .85 for 117 schools. Effectiveness (IPOE) had a Cronbach's alpha of .90 for 117 schools. These Cronbach's alphas were high enough. Listwise, only 107 schools presenting data in all the variables were selected for statistic analyses; the rest were dropped. The numbers of samples dropped were small and had no significant effect on the Cronbach's alpha. Moreover, coefficient alpha was meant to test for the internal consistency of the scores.

References

Amor, D., Conry-Oseguera, P., Cox, M., King, N., McDonnell, L., Pascal, A., Pauly, E., & Zellman, G. (1976). *Analysis of the school preferred reading program in selected Los Angeles minority schools (Report No. R-2007-LAUSD)*. Santa Monica, CA: Rand.

Andrews, J. H. M. (1965). School organizational climate: Some validity studies. *Canadian Education and Research digest, 5*.

Andrew, R. H. (1990). The development of a learning styles program in a low socioeconomic, underachieving North Carolina elementary school. *Journal of Reading, Writing, and Learning Disabilities International, 6(3)*.

Appleberry, J. B., & Hoy, W. K. (1969). The pupil control ideology of professional personnel in 'open' and 'closed' elementary schools. *Educational Administration Quarterly, 5*.

Ashton, P. T. (1985). Motivation and the teacher's sense of efficacy. In C. Ames & R. Ames (Eds.), *Research on motivation in education: Vol. 2*. The classroom milieu (pp. 141- 174). Orlando, FL: Academic Press.

Bandura, A. (1977). Self-efficacy: Towards a unifying theory of behavioral change. *Psychological Review, 84*.

Bandura, A. (1997). Self-efficacy. The exercise of control. NY: W. H. Freeman.

Bankston, C, L, III., & Caldas, S. J. (1998). Family structure, schoolmates, and racial inequality in school achievement. *Journal of Marriage and the Family, 60*.

Bloom, B. S. (1964). *Stability and change in human characteristics.* New York: Wiley.

Bornstein, M. C., & Bradley, R. H. (Eds.) (2003). Socioeconomic status, parenting, and child development. Mahwah, NJ: Lawrence Erlbaum.

Brookover, W. B., Schweitzer, J. H., Schneider, J. M., Beady, C. H., Flood, P. K., & Wisenbaker, J. M. (1978). Elementary school social climate and school achievement. *American Educational Research Journal, 15.*

Brophy, J. E. (1983). Research on the self-fulfilling prophecy and teacher expectations. *Journal of Educational Psychology, 75.*

Bryk, A., Lee, V., & Holland, P. (1993). *Catholic schools and the common good.* Cambridge, MA: Harvard University Press.

Byrne, B. M. (1990). Self-concept and academic achievement: Investigating their importance as discriminators of academic track membership in high school. *Canadian Journal of Education, 15(2).*

Cameron, K. S., & Whetten, D. A. (1983). *Organizational effectiveness: A comparison of multiple models.* New York: Academic Press.

Campbell, J. P. (1977). On the nature of organizational effectiveness. In P.S. Goodman & J. M. Pennings (Eds.), *New Perspectives on organizational effectiveness (pp. 13- 55).* San Francisco: Jossey-Bass.

Chen, C. (1996). Long-term prediction of academic achievement of American, Chinese, and Japanese adolescents. *Journal of Education Psychology, 88(4).*

Cheng, C. Y. (1991). Organizational environment in schools: Commitment, control disengagement, and headless. *Educational Administration Quarterly, 27(4).*

Clark, R. M. (1990). Why disadvantaged students succeed: What happens outside of school is critical. *Public Welfare, 17 (A23).*

Cloer, Jr. T., & Alexander, Jr. W. (1992). Inviting teacher characteristics and teacher effectiveness. *Journal of Invitational Theory and Practice, 1.*

Coleman, J. S., Campbell, E. Q., Hobson, C. J., McPartland, J., Mood, A. M., Weinfeld, F. D. & York, R. L. (1966). Equality of educational opportunity. Washington, DC: Government Printing Office.

Corwin, R. G., & Borman, K. M. (1988). School as workplace: Structural constraints on administration. In N. J. Boyan (Ed.), *Handbook of research on educational administration (pp. 209-237).* New York: Longman.

DeBaryshe, B. D., Patterson, G. R., & Capaldi, D. M. (1993). A performance model for academic achievement in early adolescent boys. *Developmental Psychology, 29.*

Deibert, P. J., & Hoy, K. W. (1977). "Custodial" high schools and self-actualization of students. *Educational Research Quarterly, 2(2).*

Denig, S. J. (1999). Discipline in public and religious schools and self-actualization of students. *Educational Research Quarterly, 2.*

Dunn, R., Dunn, K., Primavera, L., Sinatra, R., & Virostko, J. (1987). A timely solution: Effects of chronobiology on achievement and behavior. *The Clearing House, 61,* 5-8.

Edmonds, R. R. (1979). Effective schools for the urban poor. *Educational Leadership, 37.*

Eresimadu, F. N. J. (1987). Producing effective teachers for primary school: Nigeria's case. In F. N. J. Eresimadu & G. C. Nduka (Eds.), *Readings in education.* Awka, Nigeria: Meks-Unique Publishers.

Estadt, G. J., Willower, D. J., & Caldwell, W. E. (1976). School principals' role administrative behavior and teacher pupil control behavior: A test of the Domino Theory. *Contemporary Education, 47.*

Estep, L. E., Willower, D. J., & Licata, J. W. (1980). Teacher pupil control ideology and behavior as predictors of classroom robustness. *High School Journal, 63.*

Etzioni, A. (1975). *A comparative analysis of complex organizations.* New York: Free Press.

Evans, G. W. (2004). The environment of childhood poverty. *American Psychologist, 59(2).*

Fan, X. (2001). Parental involvement and students' academic achievement: A modeling analysis. *Journal of Experimental Education, 70(1).*

Fan, X., & Chen, M. (2001). Parental involvement and students' academic achievement: A meata-analysis. *Educational Psychology Review, 13(1).*

Ferguson, R. (1998). Test score trends along racial lines, 1971 to 1996: Popular culture and community academic standards. 348-390. *America becoming: Racial trends and consequences, Vol. 1.* National Research Council, Washington, D.C., National Academy Press.

Finkelstein, R. (1999). *The effects of organizational health and pupil control ideology on the achievement and alienation of high school students.* Unpublished doctoral dissertation, St. John's University Jamaica, New York.

Forehand, G. A., & Gilmer, B. (1964). Environmental variation in studies of organizational behavior. *Psychological Bulletin, 62.*

Georgopoulos, B., & Tannenbaum, A. S. (1957). A study of organizational effectiveness. *American Sociological Review 22.*

Gilbert, D. C., & Levinson, D. J. (1957). Custodialism and humanism in mental hospital structure and staff ideology. In M. Greenblatt, D. Leveinson, & R. Williams (Eds.), *The Patient and the Mental Hospital* (pp. 20-34). Glencoe, IL: The Free Press.

Gilmer, B. (1966). *Industrial psychology.* New York: McGraw-Hill.

Glickman, C. D., Gordon, P. G., & Ross-Gordon, M. J. (2001). *Supervision and instructional leadership: A development approach.* Boston: Allyn and Bacon.

Goddard, R. D., Hoy, W. K. Hoy, A. W. (2000). Collective teacher efficacy, its meaning, impact, and measure on student achievement. American Educational Research Journal, 37(2).

Goodlad, J. (1984). *A place called schooling: Prospects for the future.* New York, NY: McGraw-Hill.

Goodman, P. S., & Pennings, J. M. (1977). Toward a workable framework. In P. S. Goodman & J. M. Pennings (Eds.), *New Perspectives on organizational effectiveness* (pp. 147-184). San Francisco: Jossey-Bass.

Gordon, D. (1997). *The relationship among academic self-concept, academic achievement, and persistence with self-attribution, study habits, and perceived school environment.* Unpublished doctoral dissertation, Purdue University, Indiana.

Gottfried, A. (1985). Measures of socioeconomic status in child development research: Data and recommendations. *Merrill-Palmer Quarterly, 31(1).*

Guskey, T. R. (1982). The effects of change in instructional effectiveness on the relationship of teacher expectations and students achievement. *Journal of educational research, 75.*

Hall, E., Hall, C., & Abaci, R. (1997). The effects of human relations training on reported teacher stress, pupil control ideology, and locus of control. *British Journal of Educational Psychology, 19.*

Halpin, A.W., & Croft, D. B. (1963). *The organizational climate of schools.* Chicago: Midwest Administration Center of the University of Chicago.

Hao, L., & Bonstead-Bruns, M. (1998). Parent-Child differences in educational expectations and the academic achievement of immigrant and native students. *Sociology of Education, 71(July).*

Hobbs, N., Dokecki, P. R., Hoover-Dempsey, K. V., Moroney, R. M., Shayne, M.W., & Weeks, K. H. (1984). *Strengthening families*. San Francisco: Jossey-Bass.

Hoover-Dempsey, K. V., & Brissie, J. S. (1987). Parent involvement: Contributions of teacher efficacy, school socioeconomic status, and other school characteristics *American Educational Research Journal, 24(3)*.

Houser, R. M. (1994). Measuring socioeconomic status in studies of child development. *Child Development, 65(6)*.

Hauser-Cram, P., Warfield, M. E., Stadler, j., & Sirin, S. R. (2005). School environments and the diverging pathways of students living in poverty. In A. Huston and M. Ripke (Eds.), Middle Childhood: Contexts of development. New Haven, CT: Cambridge University Press.

Hoy, K. W., & Clover, I. R. S. (1986). Elementary school climate: A revision of the OCDQ. *Educational Administration Quarterly, 22(1)*.

Hoy, K. W., & Henderson, E. J. (1983). Principal authenticity, school climate, and pupil-control orientation. *The Alberta Journal of Educational Research, 29(2)*.

Hoy, K. W., & Miskel, G. C. (1996). *Educational administration: Theory, research, and practice*. New York: McGraw-Hill.

Hoy, K. W., & Miskel, G. C. (2001). *Educational administration: Theory, research and practice*. Boston: McGrall-Hill.

Hoy, K. W., & Sabo, J. D. (1998). *Quality middle schools*. California: Corwin Press.

Hoy, K. W., & Sweetland, S. R. (2000). Bureaucracies that work: Enabling not coercive. *Journal of School Leadership, 10*.

Hoy, K. W., Hannum, J., & Tschannen-Moran, M. (1998). Organizational climate and student achievement: A parsimonious and longitudinal view. *Journal of School Leadership, 8*.

Hoy, W. K. (1967). Organizational socialization: The student teacher and pupil control ideology. *Journal of Educational Research, 61.*

Hoy, W. K. (2001). The pupil control studies: A historical, theoretical and empirical analysis. *Journal of Educational Administration, 39(5).*

Hoy, W. K., & Feldman, A. J. (1987). Organizational health: The concept and its measure. *Journal of Research and Development in Education, 20(4).*

Hoy, W. K., & Ferguson, J. (1985). A theoretical framework and exploration of organizational effectiveness in schools. *Educational Administration Quarterly, 21.*

Hoy, W. K., Hannum, J., Tschannen-Moran, M. (1998). Organizational climate and student achievement: A parsimonious and longitudinal view. *Journal of School Leadership, 8(4).*

Hoy, W. K., Hoffman, J., Sabo, D., & Bliss, J. R. (1996). The organizational climate of middle schools: The development and test of the OCDQ-RM. *Journal of Educational Administration, 34.*

Smith, P. A., Hoy, K. W., & Sweetland, S. R. (2003). The development of organizational climate index for high schools: Its measure and relationship to faculty trust. *The High School Journal, 86(2).*

Hoy, W. K., Tarter, C. J., & Bliss, J. (1990). Organizational climate, school health, and effectiveness: A comparative analysis. *Educational Administration Quarterly, 26.*

Hoy, W. K., Tarter, C. J., & Wiskowskie, L. (1992). Faculty trust in colleagues: Linking the principal with school effectiveness. *Journal of Research and Development in Education, 26(1).*

Hoy, W. K., Tarter, J. C., & Forsyth, P. (1978). Administrative behavior and subordinate loyalty: An empirical assessment. *Journal of Educational Administration, 16(1).*

Hoy, W. K., Tatar, C. J., & Kottkamp, B. R. (1991). *Open schools/ Healthy schools: Measuring organizational climate.* Newbury Park: Sage Publications.

Hoy, W. K., & Woolfolk, A. E. (1993). Teachers' sense of efficacy and the organizational health of schools. *The Elementary School Journal, 93(4).*

Kannapel, P. J., & Clements, S. K., with Taylor, D., & Hibpshman, T. (2005). *Inside the black box of high-performing high-poverty schools. Lexington, KY: Prichard Committee for Academic Excellence.* Retrieved March 18, 2012 from http://people.uncw.edu/kozloffm/highperforminghighpoverty.pdf

Keefe, J. W. (1982). Assessing student learning styles: An overview. In J. W. Keefe (Ed.), *Student Learning Styles and Behavior (pp. 43-53).* Reston, VA: National Association of Secondary School Principals.

Kerman, S., & Martin, M. (1980). *Teacher expectations and student achievement: Teacher handbook.* Downey, CA: Los Angeles County Superintendent of Schools.

Kimston, D. R., & Sonnabend, C. L. (1975). Public secondary schools: The interrelationships between organizational health and innovativeness and between organizational health and staff characteristics. *Urban Education, 10(1).*

Kober, N. (2001, April). *It takes more than testing: Closing the achievement gap.* A report of the Center on Education Policy. Washington, DC: Center on Education Policy.

Kottkamp, B. R., Mulhern, J. A., and Hoy, K. W. (1987). Secondary school climate: A review of the OCDQ. *Educational Administration Quarterly, 23(3).*

Kottkamp, R. B., & Mulhern, J. A. (1987). Teacher expectance motivation, open to closed climate and pupil control ideology in high schools. *Journal of Research and Development in Education, 20.*

Ladson-Billings, G. (1994). The dreamkeepers: Successful teachers of African American children. San Francisco, CA: Jossey-Bass

Lareau, A. (1987). Social class differences in family-school relationships: The importance of cultural capital. *Sociology of Education, 60.*

Lee, V. E., & Smith, J. B. (1999). Social support and achievement for young adolescents in Chicago: The role of school academic press. *American Educational Research Journal, 36(4).*

Litwin, G. H., & Stringer, R. A., Jr. (1968). *Motivation and organizational climate.* Boston: Harvard University Press.

Lunenburg, C. F. (1983). Pupil control ideology and self-concept as a learner. *Educational Research Quarterly, 8(3).*

Lunenburg, C. F. (1984). *Pupil control in schools: Individual and organizational correlates.* Lexington, MA: Ginn and Company.

Lunenburg, F. C., & Schmidt, L. J. (1989). Pupil control ideology, pupil control behavior and the quality of school life. *Journal of Research and Development in Education, 22(4).*

Lytton, H., & Pyryt, M. (1998). Predictors of achievement in basic skill: A Canadian effective schools study. *Canadian Journal of Education, 23.*

Ma, X., & Klinger, D. A. (2000). Hierarchical linear modeling of student and school effects on academic achievement. *Canadian Journal of Education, 25(1).*

Madaus, G. F., Airasian, P. W., & Kellaghan, T. (1980). *School effectiveness: A reassessment of the evidence.* New York: McGraw-Hill.

Matthews, D. B. (1991). The effects of learning styles on grade of first-year college students. *Research in Higher Education, 32(3).*

Mboya, M. M. (1988). A comparative analysis of the self-concept and academic achievement of black and white high-school students. *School Psychology International, 9(3).*

McLoyd, V. C., & Duke, U. (1998). Socioeconomic disadvantage and child development. *American Psychologist, 53(2)*.

McNeal Jr., & Ralph, B. (2001). Differential effects of parental involvement on cognitive and behavioral outcomes by socioeconomic status. *Journal of Socio-Economics, 30(2)*.

Miles, M. B. (1965). Education and innovation: The organization in context. In M. Abbott and J. Lovell (Eds.), *Changing perspectives in educational administration (pp. 54-72)*. Auburn, Al: Auburn University.

Miles, M. B. (1969). Planned change and organizational health: Figure and ground. In F. D. Carver & T. J. Sergiovanni (Eds.), *Organizations and human behavior (pp. 375 – 391)*. New York: McGraw-Hill.

Miller, C. D., Always, M., & McKinley, D. L. (1987). Effects of learning styles and strategies on academic success. *Journal of college student personnel, 28(5)*.

Mintzberg, H. (1978). Pattern in strategy formation. *Management Science, 24*.

Mintzberg, H. (1989). *Mintzberg on Management*. New York: Free Press.

Miskel, C., Fevurly, R., & Stewart, J. (1979). Organizational structures and processes, perceived school effectiveness, loyalty, and job satisfaction. *Educational Administration Quarterly, 15*.

Miskel, C., McDonald, D., & Bloom, S. (1983). Structural and expectance linkages within schools and organizational effectiveness. *Educational Administration Quarterly, 19*.

Mott, P. E. (1972). *The characteristics of effective organizations*. NY: Harper and Row.

Mouzelis, P. N. (1967). *Organization and Bureaucracy: An analysis of modern theories*. New York: Aldine Pub.

Mueller, C. W., & Parcel, T. L. (1981). Measures of socioeconomic status: Alternatives and recommendations. *Child Development, 52.*

Murphy, J., Weil, M., Hallinger, P., & Mitman, A. (1982). Academic press: Translating high expectations into school policies and classroom practices. *Educational Leadership, 40.*

Nadler, D. A., & Tushman, M. L. (1989). Organizational frame bending: Principles for managing reorientation. *Academy of Management Executive, 3.*

Nashtscheim, N., & Hoy, W. K. (1976). Authoritarian personality and control ideologies of teachers. *The Alberta Journal of Educational Research, 22.*

Nwankwo, I. J. (1979). The school climate as a factor in students' conflict behavior in Nigeria. *Educational Studies, 10(3).*

O'Day, J., & Bitter, C. (2003, June). *Evaluation study of the immediate intervention/underperforming schools program and the high achieving/improving schools program of the Public Schools Accountability Act of 1999.* Final report. Sacramento, CA: California Department of Education, Policy and Evaluation.

Pace, C. R., & Stern, G. C. (1958). An approach to the measure of Psychological characteristics of college environments. *Journal of Educational Psychology, 49.*

Pajares, F. (1996). Self-efficacy beliefs in academic settings. *Review of Educational Research, 66.*

Parsons, T. (1960). *Structure and process in modern societies.* New York: Free Press.

Parsons, T. (1967). Some ingredients of a general theory of formal organization. In A. W. Halpin (Ed.), *Administrative theory in education (pp. 40 – 72).* New York: Macmillan.

Parsons, T., Bales, R. F., & Shils, E. A. (1953). *Working papers in the theory of action.* Illinois : Free Press.

Phillips, M. (1997). What makes schools effective: A comparison of the relationships of communitarian climate and academic climate to mathematics achievement and attendance in middle school. *American Educational Research Journal, 34.*

Raudenbush, S. W. (1984). Magnitude of teacher expectancy effects on pupil IQ as a function of the credibility of expectancy induction: A synthesis of findings from 18 experiments. *Journal of Educational Psychology, 76.*

Rokeach, M. (1960). *The open and closed mind.* New York: Basic Books.

Rose, L. C., Gallup, A. M., & Elam, S. M. (1997). The 29th Annual Phi Delta Kappa/Gallup Poll of the Public's attitude toward the Public Schools. *Phi Delta Kappan, 79.*

Rosenholtz, S. J. (1985). Political myths about educational reform: Lessons from research on teaching. *Phi Delta Kappan, 65.*

Rosenthal, R., & Jacobs, L. (1968). *Pygmalion in the classroom: Teacher expectation and pupils' intellectual development.* NY: Holt, Rinehart and Winston.

Ross, J. A. (1992). Teacher efficacy and the effect of coaching of student achievement. *Canadian Journal of Education, 17(1).*

Rotter, J. B. (1966). Generalized expectancies of internal versus external control of reinforcement. *Psychological Monographs, 80(1).*

Schmidt, L. J., & Jacobson, M. H. (1990). *Pupil control in the school climate.* (ERIC Document Reproduction Service No. ED319692).

Scott, W. R. (1992). *Organizations: Rational, natural, and open systems* (3rd. ed.). New Jersey: Prentice Hall.

Scott, W. R. (1998). *Organizations: Rational, natural, and open systems* (4th. ed.). New Jersey: Prentice Hall.

Sergiovanni, T. J. (1992). *Moral leadership: Getting to the heart of school improvement.* San Francisco: Jossey-Bass.

Sherif, M. (1961). *In common predicament: Social Psychology of intergroup conflict and cooperation.* Boston: Houghton Mifflin.

Silberman, E. E. (1970). *Crisis in the classroom.* New York: Random House.

Silver, P. (1983). Educational administration: *Theoretical perspectives in practice and research.* New York: Harper and Row.

Sirin, S. R. (2005). Socioeconomic status and academic achievement: A meta-analytic review of research. *Review of Educational Research, 75(3).*

Skaalvik, E. M., & Skaalvik, S. (2004). Self-concept and self-efficacy: A test of the internal/external frame of reference model and predictions of subsequent motivation and achievement. *Psychological Reports, 95.*

Smith, P. A., Hoy, W. K., & Sweetland, S. R. (2003). Organizational health of high schools and dimensions of faculty trust. *Journal of School Leadership, 11.*

Steers, R. M. (1977). *Organizational effectiveness: A behavioral view.* Santa Monica, CA: Goodyear.

Stewart, D. (1979). A critique of school climate: What it is, how it can be improved and some general recommendations. *The Journal of Educational Administration, 17(2).*

St. John, N. (1970). The validity of children's report of their parents' educational level: A methodological note. *Sociology of Education, 43.*

Tagiuri, R. (1968). The concept of organizational climate. In R. Tagiuri & G. H. Litwin (Eds.), *Organizational climate: Explorations of a concept (pp. 1-32).* Boston: Harvard University.

Tarter, C. J., Sabo, D., & Hoy, W. K. (1995). Middle school climate, faculty trust, and effectiveness: A path analysis. *Journal of Research and Development in Education ,29.*

Tarter, J. C., Hoy, K. W., & Bliss, J. (1989). Principal leadership and organizational commitment: the principal must deliver. *Planning and Changing, 20(3)*.

Taylor, D. E. (2008). The influence of climate on student achievement in elementary schools. (Doctoral dissertation, The George Washington University). Retrieved on March 18, 2012 from Proquest Dissertations. (UMI No. 3297071).

Thompson, D. E., Orr, B., Thompson, C., & Park, O. (2002). Preferred learning styles of postsecondary technical institute instructors. *Journal of Industrial Teacher Education, 39(4)*.

Tschannen-Moran, M., & Barr, M. (2004). Fostering student learning: The relationship of collective teacher efficacy and student achievement. *Leadership and Policy in Schools, 3(3)*.

U.S. Department of Education (2001a). *Longitudinal Evaluation of School Change and Performance (LESCP) in Title I schools, Volume 1: Executive summary* (Doc. No. 2001 -20). Washington, DC: Office of the Deputy Secretary.

Walberg, H. J. (1984). Improving the productivity of America's schools. *Educational Leadership, 41(8)*.

Walberg, H. J., & Paik, S. J. (2000). *Effective educational practices*. Educational practices series – 3. Switzerland: PCL, Lausanne.

Weller, W. (1932). *The sociology of teaching*. New York: Wiley.

White, K. R. (1982). The relation between socioeconomic status and academic achievement. *Psychological Bulletin, 91(3)*.

Willower, D. J. (1965). Hypotheses on the school as a social system. *Educational Administration Quarterly, 1*.

Willower, D. J., & Jones, R. G., (1963). When pupil control becomes an institutional theme. *Phi Delta Kappan, 45*.

Willower, D. J., & Landis, C. A. (1970). Pupil control ideology and professional orientation of school faculty. *Journal of Secondary Education, 45*.

Willower, D. J., Eidell, T. L., & Hoy, W. K. (1967). *The school and pupil control ideology.* University Park: Pennsylvania State University.

Wilson, W. J. (1996). *When work disappears: The world of the new urban poor.* New York: Alfred A. Knopf.